Contents

1	Introduction	2
2	Gains from Trade	13
3	Supply and Demand	27
4	Equilibrium	66
5	Elasticity	94
6	Taxes and Subsidies	112
8	Price Controls	143
10	Externalities	160
11	Costs and Profit Maximization	177
13	Monopoly	219
15	Oligopoly	241

Chapter 1
Introduction

Chapter 1: The Ideas of Economics
Principles of Microeconomics

Prof. Greg Madonia

California State University, Chico

Outline

1. What is Economics?

2. The Ideas of Economics

3. Math Basics

What is Economics?

> **Definition: Economics**
>
> A social science that studies the choices that people make to attain their goals, given their scarce resources

Sciences
- Natural
  - Physics, chemistry, biology,...
- Social
  - **Economics**, sociology, psychology,...
- Formal
  - Mathematics, logic,...

- Natural sciences study natural phenomena
- Social sciences study human behavior
- Formal sciences use prior knowledge to advance theories
- Both the natural and social sciences use empirical studies to test their theories about how the world works

What is Economics?

Micro vs. Macro

- **Microeconomics (✓)**
  - Focuses on individuals
    - People, firms,...
  - Seeks to answer the questions of:
    1. What to produce?
    2. How much to produce?
    3. Who receives the goods produced?
- ~~Macroeconomics~~
  - Study of the economy as a whole
  - Study of
    - economic growth, unemployment, inflation, and income distribution

Now let's look at some of the **key principles** we can rely on throughout the semester

---

The Ideas of Economics

Idea 1: Incentives Matter

> **Definition: Incentives**
>
> Rewards and penalties that induce an economic agent to act

- People respond to incentives
  - Examples: Money, duty, love, hate, power, reputation

- Responses are predictable

Idea 2: Self-interest and Social Interest Align Under Good Institutions

- Institutions – rules and norms
    - Property rights
    - Legal system
    - Stable government
    - **Markets**

- Well functioning markets $\implies$ alignment

- "Invisible Hand"

- Governments can improve market outcomes when markets fail

Idea 3: Trade-offs Exist and Are Everywhere

- Post-high school diploma (or GED) decision
    - How much more education to get if any?
    - Benefits: knowledge, higher wages
    - Costs: tuition, wages you could earn

- Legal system
    - Higher burden of proof
    - Benefit: More innocent people go free
    - Cost: More guilty people go free

Idea 3: Trade-offs Exist and Are Everywhere

> **Definition: Scarcity**
>
> The amount of resources is less than the amount needed to satisfy all wants

- Scarcity $\implies$ trade-off
    - Something gained and something lost

- That loss can be measured measured/evaluated

> **Definition: Opportunity Cost**
>
> The value of the next-best alternative

- What is the cost of being here today?

Idea 3: Trade-offs Exist and Are Everywhere

- Scarcity
    - $\implies$ choices matter
    - $\implies$ things have value
    - $\implies$ this course (... and discipline)

- The "Big Economic Question"
    - How can we best use our scarce resources?

Idea 4: Rational People Think on the Margin

- We will assume people are rational

- **Marginal** means additional
  - One more/less

- Rational agents will take an action **if and only if**

$$\text{marginal benefit} > \text{marginal cost}$$

Idea 5: Trade *Can* Make People Better Off

- Generalized version of trade: unambiguous benefits

- Trade allows people to do what they do best
  - Specialization $\implies$ **more production**

- Without trade everyone would have to make everything they consume

- International trade is more complicated

Idea 6: Economic Growth is Important to Make People Better Off

- Economic growth $\implies$ increases in wealth
- Wealth and happiness are positively correlated

Figure: Life Satisfaction and GDP per capita

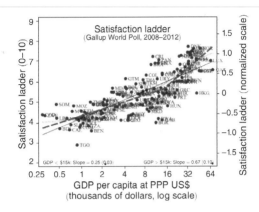

Source: Stevenson and Wolfers (American Economic Review, 2013)

Idea 7: Well Functioning Institutions Matter

- Institutions allow people to invest

- Institutions
    - Property rights
    - Legal system
    - Political stability
    - Well functioning markets

Ch. 1: Introduction
└─ The Ideas of Economics
   └─ Idea 7: Well Functioning Institutions Matter

- "Investments" are more general than financial investments
  - Human capital is the acquisition of skills on an individual level
  - Research and development

Remaining Ideas

▶ Idea 8: Economic Booms and Busts Are Inevitable, But Can Be Mitigated

▶ Idea 9: Increases in the Money Supply Can Lead to Inflation

▶ Idea 10: Managing the Macroeconomy Is Hard

Critical Math Concepts

Functions ▸ more info

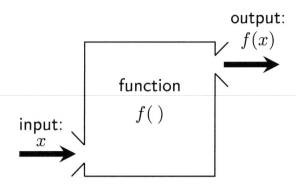

- ▶ A function taxes an input, x, and turns it into an output, $f(x)$
    - ◇ Needs to turn x into only one $f(x)$ for it to be a valid function
- ▶ Important for this class:
    - ◇ Equation of a straight line

$$y = mx + b$$

Critical Math Concepts

Equation of a Line ▸ more info

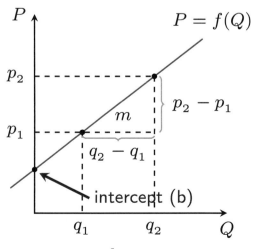
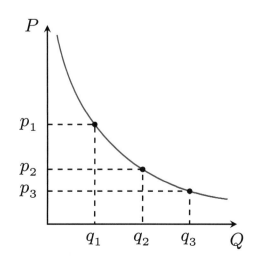

- ▶ $p = mq + b$
- ▶ slope (m)

$$m = \frac{\Delta p}{\Delta q} = \frac{p_{\text{new}} - p_{\text{old}}}{q_{\text{new}} - q_{\text{old}}}$$

Critical Math Concepts

Percent Change ▶ more info

$$\%\Delta = \frac{x_{\text{new}} - x_{\text{old}}}{x_{\text{old}}} \times 100$$

Suppose $x_1 = 100$ and $x_2 = 50$

▶ $x_1 \longrightarrow x_2$
$$\%\Delta = \frac{50 - 100}{100} \times 100 = -50\%$$

▶ $x_2 \longrightarrow x_1$
$$\%\Delta = \frac{100 - 50}{50} \times 100 = +100\%$$

Critical Math Concepts

Area

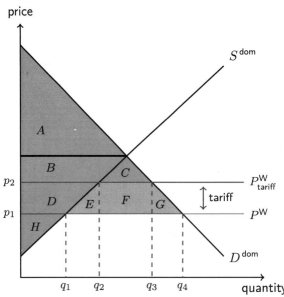

▶ area of E = area(*triangle*) = $\frac{1}{2}bh = \frac{1}{2}(q_2 - q_1)(p_2 - p_1)$
▶ area of F = area(*rectangle*) = $bh = (q_3 - q_2)(p_2 - p_1)$

Chapter 2

Gains from Trade

Chapter 2: Comparative Advantage and the Gains from Trade
Principles of Microeconomics

Prof. Greg Madonia

California State University, Chico

Outline

1. Economics as a Science

2. Production Possibilities Frontier (PPF)
   - Opportunity Cost

3. The Gains from Trade
   - A Stylized Example
   - Specialization in Practice

Economics as a Science

Economics is a *social science* that uses empirical methods to test its theories

- ▶ Scientific Method

- ▶ Experiments to test a theory
    - ◇ Difficult to do
    - ◇ Are the results meaningful?

- ▶ Observation
    - ◇ Natural experiments

Economic Models

- ▶ Economists build/use models to help understand the "real world"

- ▶ Trade-off
    - ◇ Focus on important relationships
    - ◇ Omit many details via assumptions

- ▶ Change assumptions
    - ◇ Different results ...maybe

- ▶ Our first model...

Production Possibilities Frontier (PPF)

▶ PPF shows the combinations of output that the economy ___
  _____

▶ Assumptions of this model:
  1.

▶ Variables in this model:
  1. Factors of production (inputs)
     1.1
     1.2

  2. Technology
     - How inputs are are transformed into output

Our First PPF Model

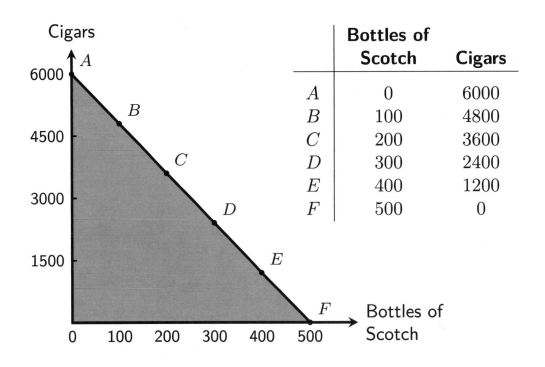

	Bottles of Scotch	Cigars
A	0	6000
B	100	4800
C	200	3600
D	300	2400
E	400	1200
F	500	0

What Can the PPF Tell Us?

Is the economy behaving efficiently?

1. **Efficient levels of production**
   - Getting the most out of its scarce resources
   - Points _____ are efficient
     ◇ Trade-offs
2. **Inefficient levels of production**
   - Points _____ of the PPF (no trade-off necessary)
3. **Impossible levels of production**
   - Points _____

The slope of the PPF can tell us something about the **trade-off** between the two goods...

Opportunity Cost

Definition: Opportunity Cost

The highest-valued alternative that _____ to engage in an activity

- Slope of the PPF tells us the **opportunity cost** of producing either good

	Bottles of Scotch	Cigars
A	0	6000
B	100	4800
C	200	3600
D	300	2400
E	400	1200
F	500	0

$D \longrightarrow E$:
- gain ____ bottles of scotch, **but**
- have to give up ____ cigars
- $\implies$, the **opportunity cost** of those 100 bottles of scotch is

_____

17

Changing the PPF

The PPF is a Function of Two Variables

1. Resources
   ◇ Labor, capital, land, raw materials, etc...

2. Technology
   ◇ How inputs are turned into outputs

▶ These variables can
   ◇ Increase – more resources and/or technology advances, or
   ◇ Decrease – fewer resources and/or technology declines (?)

Changes in Resources/Technology

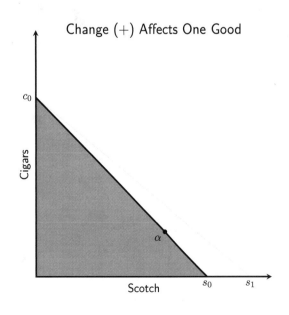
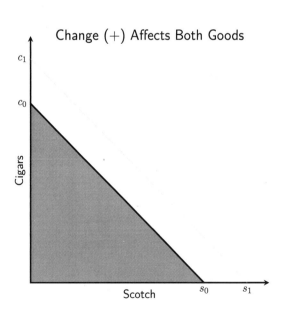

Setup

▶ Assumption: There are only two goods
  ◇ Burgers
  ◇ Donuts

▶ Assumption: There are only two people/economic agents
  ◇ Bob (cook)
  ◇ Duncan (baker)
  ◇ Each agent can make both goods

Preview of the Results

▶ If Bob spends all of this time cooking and Duncan spends all of his time baking
  ◇ Both can be better off by trading than on their own

▶ If Bob spends his day dividing time between both tasks and Duncan does the same
  ◇ Both can **specialize** in one task
  ◇ Then engage in trade and be better off than on their own

▶ We will use the PPF model to show why this is true

Duncan and Bob's PPFs

	Minutes need to make 1		Amount made in 8 hours	
	Burger	Donut	Burgers	Donuts
Duncan	30	10	16	48
Bob	15	30	32	16

▶ Both tables give similar information, but both are useful
  ◊ "Minutes needed to make X" $\implies$ opportunity cost is constant
  ◊ "Amount made in X hours" – easy to make figures

Ch. 2: Comparative Advantage
└ The Gains from Trade
  └ A Stylized Example
    └ Duncan and Bob's PPFs

- For the "Amount made in X hours":
  – Each "cell" of the table represents how much can be produced if they only do that one task for the entire time
- For Duncan
  – 30 minutes per burger $\implies$ in 8 hours 16 burgers can be made
  – 10 minutes per donut $\implies$ in 8 hours 48 donuts can be made
- For Bob
  – 15 minutes per burger $\implies$ in 8 hours 32 burgers can be made
  – 30 minutes per donut $\implies$ in 8 hours 16 donuts can be made

PPFs and Consumption without Trade

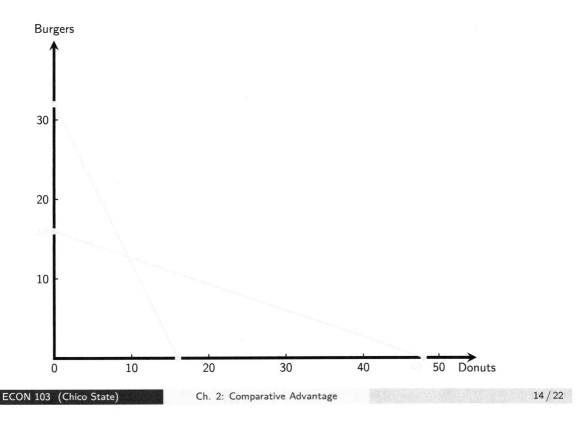

Notes for the Above Figure

	Amount made in 8 hours	
	Burgers	Donuts
Duncan	16	48
Bob	32	16

▶ Some arbitrary level of production & consumption w/o trade
  ◇ Duncan: 24 donuts and 8 burgers
  ◇ Bob: 4 donuts and 24 burgers

Specialization and Trade

▶ Bob should specialize in cooking burgers
  ◇ More time cooking burgers
  ◇ Less time making donuts

▶ Duncan should specialize in making donuts
  ◇ Less time cooking burgers
  ◇ More time making donuts

▶ Trade: 8 burgers for 16 donuts

▶ Both gain from specialization and trade

Calculating the Gains from Trade

Amount made in 8 hours

	Burgers	Donuts
Duncan	16	48
Bob	32	16

▶ Trade 8 burgers for 16 donuts

	Bob (Cook) Donuts	Bob (Cook) Burgers	Duncan (Baker) Donuts	Duncan (Baker) Burgers
Without Trade:				
Production and Consumption	4	24	24	8
With Specialization and Trade:				
Specialized Production	0	32		
Trade	Gets 16	Gives 8		
Consumption				
Gains from Trade:				
Increase in Consumption				

Visualizing the Gains from Trade

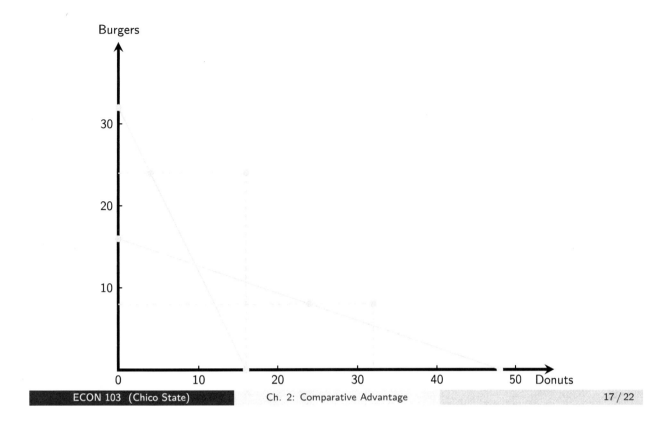

Notes for the Above Figure

▶ After specialization and trade, both Bob and Duncan are consuming outside their own PPF

Who Should Do What?

Definition: Absolute Advantage

Producing a good using _____ than another producer **OR** producing more of a good than another producer using the _____ _____

	Amount made in 8 hours	
	Burgers	Donuts
Duncan	16	48
Bob	32	16

▶ Q: Should we base our production/specialization decisions on absolute advantage?

Who Should Do What?

We should base our production/specialization decisions on comparative advantage

Definition: Comparative Advantage

The ability to produce a good at a _____ than another producer

▶ Comparative advantage reflects the relative opportunity cost

Definition: Principle of Comparative Advantage

Each good is produced by the individual that has the smaller opportunity cost of producing that good

Comparative Advantage

- One person
  - _____ have the absolute advantage in both goods
  - _____ have the comparative advantage in both goods

- For different opportunity costs
  - _____ has the comparative advantage in one good
  - _____ has the comparative advantage in the other good

- The opportunity cost of one good is the inverse (reciprocal) of the opportunity cost of the other

- Gains from specialization and trade are based on comparative advantage
  - Total production _____

- Price of trade must lie _____ the two opportunity costs

- The increase in total production, generated by people doing the "right" tasks, is what allows people to consume outside their own PPF
- If the price does not lie between the two agents opportunity costs of producing some good, then one of the agents is better-off producing both goods on their own
  - see the Blackboard example for how this works

Recipe for a Comparative Advantage Problem

1. Figure out the opportunity cost of producing both goods for both economic agents
    1.1 This is equivalent to finding out who has the comparative advantage in producing a good

2. If there is a difference in opportunity costs then there is a basis for specialization and trade

3. Each agent should specialize in producing the good for which they have the comparative advantage

4. Verify that the trading price is between the two opportunity costs

Blackboard Example

▶ Refer to the "Gains From Trade" handout (available on Blackboard)

Chapter 3

Supply and Demand

Chapter 3: Market Forces: Supply and Demand
Principles of Microeconomics

Prof. Greg Madonia

California State University, Chico

Outline

1. Markets and Competition

2. Demand
   - Marginal Benefit
   - Consumer Surplus
   - Changes in Demand

3. Supply
   - Marginal Cost
   - Producer Surplus
   - Changes in Supply

4. Wrap-up

Markets and Competition

What is a Market?

▶ A group of buyers and sellers for a _____ good or service
  ◇ Example:
    • Market for
    • Market for

▶ Buyers determine demand

▶ Sellers determine supply

Markets and Competition

Characteristics of a Market: Initial Assumptions

▶ Many buyers and sellers
  ◇ No single entity can affect price
    • "too small"

  ◇

▶ Interaction of buyers and sellers determine market outcome (much more later)
  ◇ ~~Labor Theory of Value~~

Demand

▶ Determined by buyers

Definition: Quantity Demanded

Amount of a good or service that buyers are *willing and able* to purchase _____

Definition: Demand

A _____ between prices and quantity demanded

▶ Function
▶ Represented by: tables, figures, equations

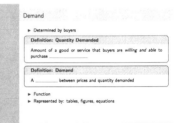

- Quantity Demanded and Demand are not the same thing
- Quantity Demanded is some number. For example: 6 apples
- Demand is the mapping of price to a quantity demanded, or vice-versa
- Note for those that have had a little more experience with math than is necessary for this course: we will only be dealing with 1-1 functions, so we can reverse the input and output of those functions (that is, their inverses)
    - A 1-1 function is a function for which there is exactly one output for each input, and vice-versa

Demand Schedule and Corresponding Demand Curve

Market for Vinyl Records

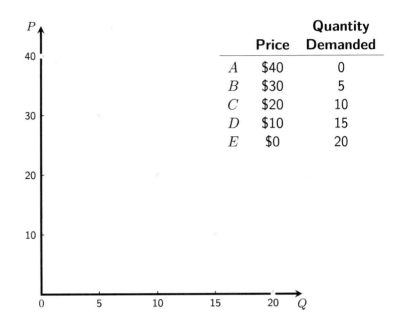

	Price	Quantity Demanded
A	$40	0
B	$30	5
C	$20	10
D	$10	15
E	$0	20

Notes for Demand Schedule and Corresponding Demand Curve

Reading Demand

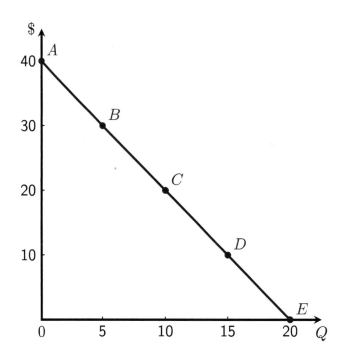

Notes for Reading Demand

- ▶ Reading horizontally
    - ◇ Given a price, how much are consumers willing and able to buy?
    - ◇ $p = \$20 \implies$
- ▶ Reading vertically
    - ◇ Given a quantity, how much are consumers willing and able to pay?
    - ◇ $q_d = 15 \implies$

Law of Demand

> **Definition: Law of Demand**
>
> Holding other things constant, when the price of a good _____ the quantity demanded of that good _____ and vice-versa

▶ $\implies$ Demand curve is _____ sloped*

▶ Demand helps describe how consumers intend to use a good, given
  1. Their preferences
  2. The possibilities to find alternatives

Notes for Law of Demand

Law of Demand: Example

► Households and the Market for Energy

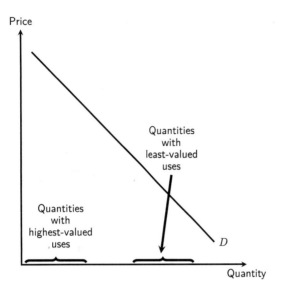

► When prices are high, households only buy a little energy and use it for their most-valued applications
  ◇ Examples?

► When prices are low, households will buy a lot of energy and even use it for their least-valued applications
  ◇ Examples?

Demand Curve Shapes

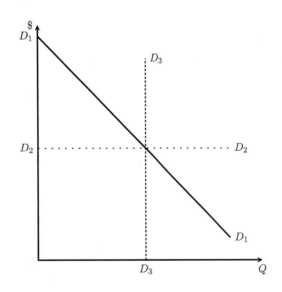
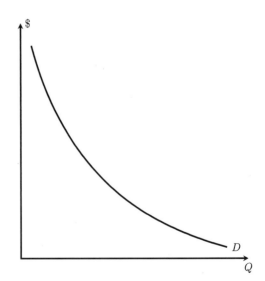

Marginal Benefit

> **Definition: Marginal Benefit** (MB)
>
> The _____ benefit to a consumer from consuming one more unit of a good or service

▶ Marginal benefit is equal to the price that you are willing to pay (*WTP*) for one more unit

　◇ Assume that a rational consumer is willing to pay for a good or service up until $MB =$

　　• The quantity where _____ is a point of indifference for the consumer

Marginal Benefit

▶ The marginal benefit curve is:
　◇ **identical** to the demand curve ($MB = D$)

　◇ **identical** to the willingness-to-pay (*WTP*) function ($MB = WTP$)
　　• WTP represents the maximum you would pay for a unit

　◇ measured in dollars

Marginal Benefit and Total Benefit

▶ Adding up the marginal benefit equals the total benefit

Unit #	MB	Total Benefit (running total)
1	12	
2	10	
3	8	

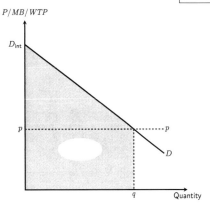

▶ Total benefit is represented by the area _____ the demand curve for the quantity consumed

---

Ch. 3: Supply and Demand
└─ Demand
 └─ Marginal Benefit
  └─ Marginal Benefit and Total Benefit

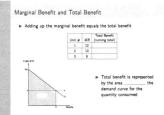

- For our purposes, whenever you hear the word "marginal" you should automatically associate that with the word "additional"
- We will assume that consumers purchase a good if the $MB = p$ of that unit
- "Adding up the marginal benefit equals the total benefit"
  – Math version (discrete quantities):

$$\text{Total Benefit} = \sum_{i=1}^{n} MB(q_i)_i$$

where n represents the number of units consumed

Consumer Surplus

> **Definition: Consumer Surplus** (CS)
>
> The amount that a buyer is willing to pay for a good minus the amount that the buyer actually pays.
>
> **For an individual quantity:**
>
> $$CS_i = MB_i - p$$
>
> **For all quantities consumed:**
>
> $$CS = CS_1 + CS_2 + CS_3 + \cdots$$
>
> this will sometimes be referred to as total consumer surplus

- CS is the _____ of consumption
- Area below the demand curve (MB) and above the price (p)

Notes for Consumer Surplus

Consumer Surplus – Visually

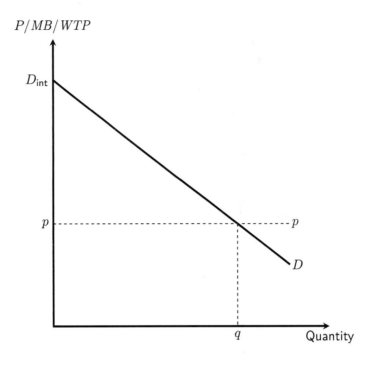

Notes for Consumer Surplus – Visually

- ▶ CS is the area under the demand curve and above the price for the quantities that are consumed.
- ▶ For the figure to the left:

$$CS =$$

- ◇ D_{int} is the demand intercept
- ◇ p is the price
- ▶ The CS for the qth quantity is zero
  - ◇ All of the quantities to the left of q have CS greater than zero

Demand Shifters

▶ Law of Demand says "Holding other things constant..."

▶ What are we holding constant?
  ◇ Variables that _____ between price and quantity
    • Shift/affect demand

▶ The variables that shift the demand curve
  ◇ P.I.N.T.E.

  ◇ **NOT** the price of the good/service in question
    • Movement along the current demand curve

Notes for Demand Shifters

An Increase in Demand

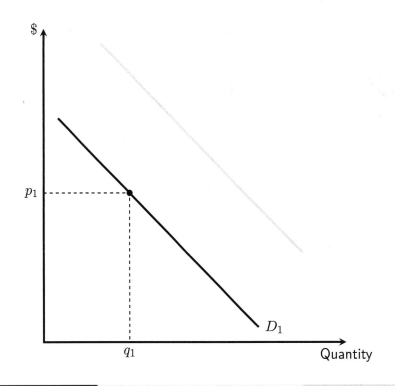

Notes for An Increase in Demand

- Demand curve shifts

- At each price, quantity demanded

- At each quantity, the *MB/WTP*

A Decrease in Demand

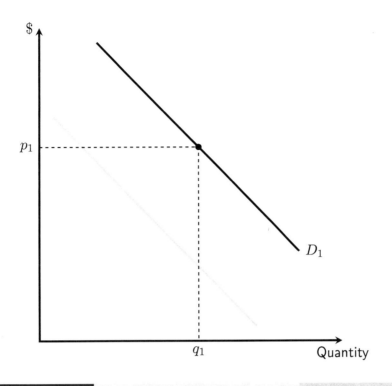

Notes for A Decrease in Demand

- ▶ Demand curve shifts

- ▶ At each price, quantity demanded

- ▶ At each quantity, the *MB/WTP*

41

P.i.n.t.e. – Prices of *Related* Goods

▶ **Prices of Substitutes**
  ◇ Example: Chicken and Steak
  ◇ Price of Good B $\implies$ Demand for Good A

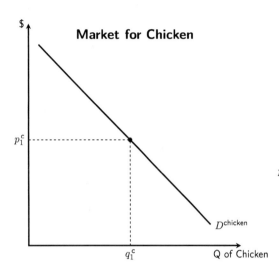
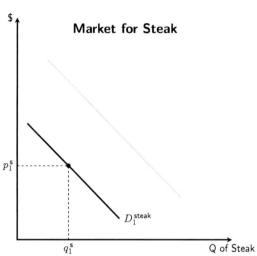

Notes for P.i.n.t.e. – Prices of *Related* Goods

P.i.n.t.e. – Prices of *Related* Goods

▶ **Prices of Complements**
  ◇ Example: Peanut Butter and Jelly
  ◇ Price of Good B ⟹ Demand for Good A

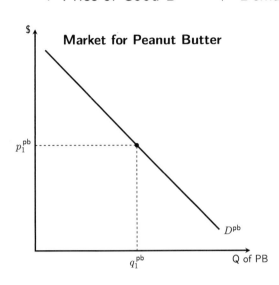
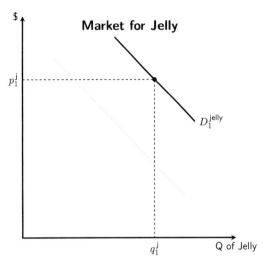

Notes for P.i.n.t.e. – Prices of *Related* Goods

p.I.n.t.e. – Income

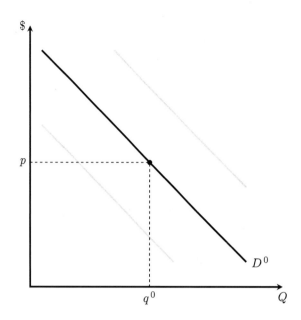

Notes for p.I.n.t.e. – Income

▶ Suppose Income ↑ ⟹ D ?
  ◇

▶
  ◇
  ◇

▶
  ◇
  ◇

p.i.N.T.e. – Number of Consumers & Tastes and Preferences

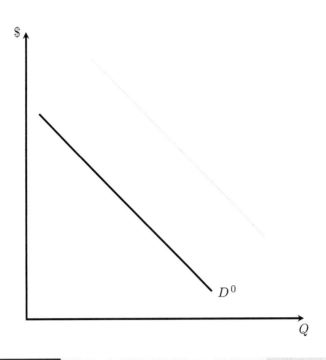

Notes for p.i.N.T.e. – Number of Consumers & Tastes and Preferences

▶ **Number of Consumers**
- Example: Demand for bread in 1880 vs. today
- Number of consumers $\uparrow \implies D$

▶ **Tastes and Preferences**
- Example: Demand for hot chocolate on June 21th vs. December 21th
- Preferences $\uparrow \implies D$

p.i.n.t.E. – Expectations about the Future

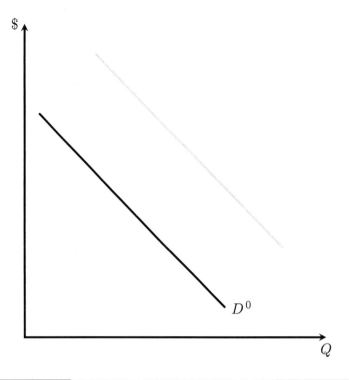

Notes for p.i.n.t.E. – Expectations about the Future

- **Expectations About Future Income**
    - Example: increase in demand for graduates from a specific major
    - Expected income $\uparrow \implies D$

- **Expectations About Future Prices**
    - Example: gasoline prices
    - Expected price $\uparrow \implies D$

Supply

▶ Determined by sellers

> **Definition: Quantity Supplied**
>
> Amount of a good or service that sellers are *willing and able* to sell
> _____

> **Definition: Supply**
>
> A _____ between prices and quantity supplied

▶ Function
▶ Represented by: tables, figures, equations

Notes for Supply

Supply Schedule and Corresponding Supply Curve

Market for Vinyl Records

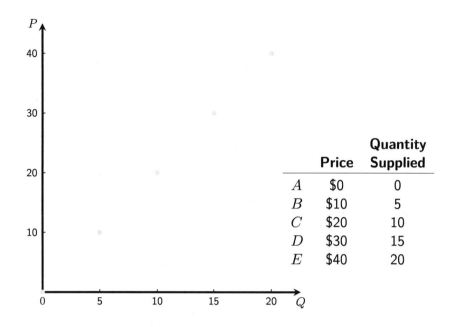

	Price	Quantity Supplied
A	$0	0
B	$10	5
C	$20	10
D	$30	15
E	$40	20

Notes for Supply Schedule and Corresponding Supply Curve

Reading Supply

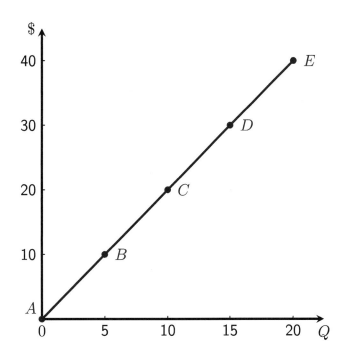

Notes for Reading Supply

▶ Reading horizontally
  ◇ Given a price, how much are sellers willing and able to provide?
  ◇ $p = \$20 \implies$

▶ Reading vertically
  ◇ Given a quantity, what price do sellers need to receive?
  ◇ $q_s = 15 \implies$

Law of Supply

> **Definition: Law of Supply**
>
> Holding other things constant, when the price of a good or service _____ the quantity supplied _____ and vice-versa

- ▶ $\implies$ Supply curve is _____ sloped*

- ▶ Supply helps describe the costs of providing a good for sellers

    1. When prices increase, sellers will produce even if costs are high

Notes for Law of Supply

Law of Supply: Example

- When prices are low, firms will use lowest-cost methods of production and provide a small amount

- When prices are high, firms will add-on higher-cost methods of production and the amount provided will increase

Supply Curve Shapes

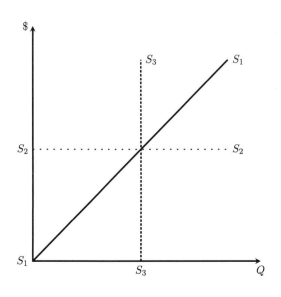
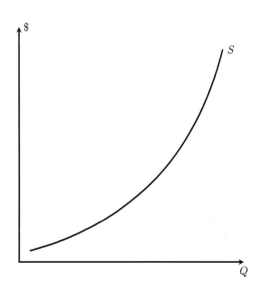

Marginal Cost

> **Definition: Cost**
>
> Value of everything the seller must give up to produce a good

▶ Measure of willingness to sell/accept

> **Definition: Marginal Cost** (MC)
>
> The _____ cost to a firm from producing one more unit of a good or service

▶ Marginal cost is equal to the _____ that you are willing to sell an additional unit of a good/service
  ◇ Assume that a rational producer is willing to give up a good or service up until, and including, the quantity where $MC =$

Marginal Cost

▶ The marginal cost curve is **highly related** to the supply curve

▶ Adding up the marginal cost of each good produced yields the total cost
  ◇ Need to assume that there are no fixed costs for this to be true

▶ Analysis of the net benefit to the producer (price - cost): **producer surplus**

Producer Surplus

Definition: Producer Surplus (PS)

The amount that a seller is paid for a good minus the seller's cost of providing it **For an individual quantity:**

$$PS_i = p - MC_i$$

For all quantities produced:

$$PS = PS_1 + PS_2 + PS_3 + \cdots$$

this will sometimes be referred to as total producer surplus

- PS is the _____ of production
- Area below the price and above the supply/MC curve

Notes for Producer Surplus

Producer Surplus – Visually

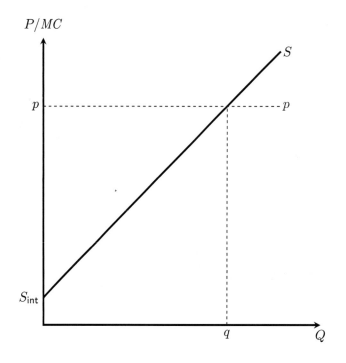

Notes for Producer Surplus – Visually

▶ PS is the area under the price and above the supply curve for the quantities that are sold.

▶ For the figure to the left:

$$PS =$$

◇ p is the price
◇ S_{int} is the supply intercept

▶ The PS for the qth quantity is zero

◇ All of the quantities to the left of q have PS greater than zero

Supply Shifters

- Law of Supply: Relationship between price and quantity supplied
  - "Holding other things constant..."

- P.I.N.T.E.
  - Changes in a P.I.N.T.E. variable changes the relationship between price and quantity supplied

- **NOT** a change in the price of the good/service itself
  - Movement along the exiting supply curve

Notes for Supply Shifters

An Increase in Supply

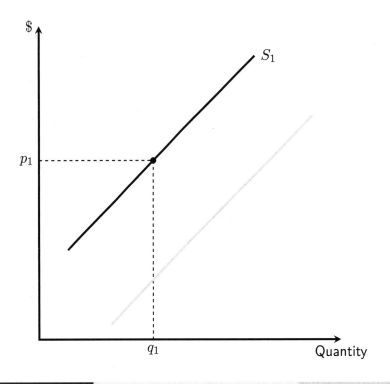

Notes for An Increase in Supply

- Supply curve shifts

- At each price, quantity supplied

- At each quantity, the MC
  - Producers will accept a _____ for the same quantity

A Decrease in Supply

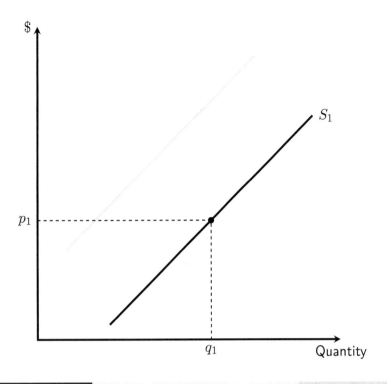

Notes for A Decrease in Supply

- Supply curve shifts

- At each price, quantity supplied

- At each quantity, the MC
    ◇ Producers will need a _____ for the same quantity

P.i.n.t.e. – Prices of Substitutes in Production

▶ **Prices of Substitutes in Production**
  ◇ Example: 2D video games
  ◇ Price of good B $\implies$ Supply of good A
  ◇ Changes in

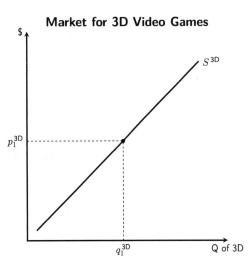
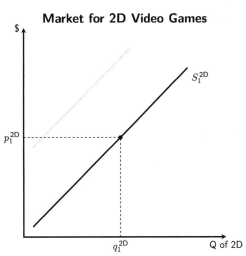

Notes for P.i.n.t.e. – Prices of Substitutes in Production

p.I.n.t.e. – Input Prices

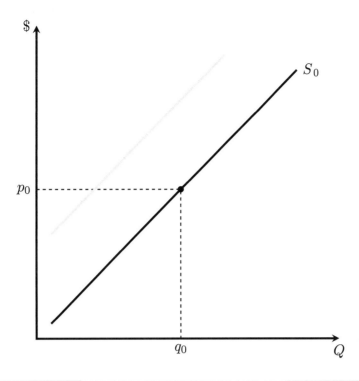

Notes for p.I.n.t.e. – Input Prices

- **Input Prices**
    - ◇ Example: Price of energy
    - ◇ Input Price $\implies$ Supply

p.I.n.t.e. – Input Prices: Taxes

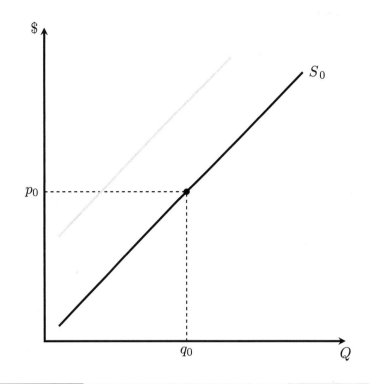

Notes for p.I.n.t.e. – Input Prices: Taxes

▶ Taxes
- Per-unit tax collected from sellers
- Same impact as
- Supply curve _____ by the amount of the tax

p.I.n.t.e. – Input Prices: Subsidies

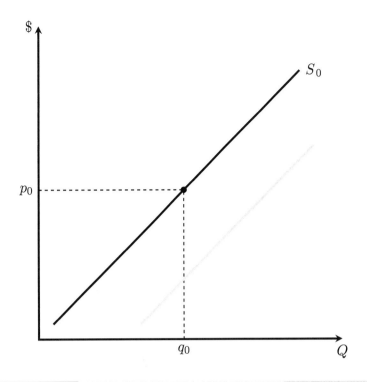

Notes for p.I.n.t.e. – Input Prices: Subsidies

▶ Subsidies
- ⋄ Per-unit payment paid to sellers
- ⋄ Same impact as
- ⋄ Supply curve _____ by the amount of the subsidy

p.i.**N**.t.e. – Number of Producers

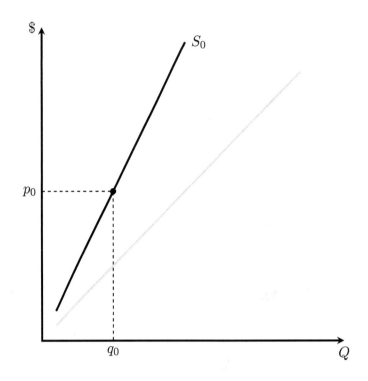

Notes for p.i.**N**.t.e. – Number of Producers

▶ **Number of Producers**
- ⋄ Example: Number of brewers in the US in 1930 vs. today
- ⋄ Number of Producers $\implies$ Supply

p.i.n.**T**.e. – Technology

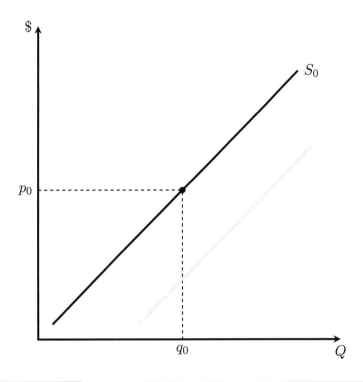

Notes for p.i.n.**T**.e. – Technology

▶ **Technology**
- ⋄ Example: Printing press
- ⋄ Technology $\implies$ Supply

p.i.n.t.E. – Expectations about Future Prices

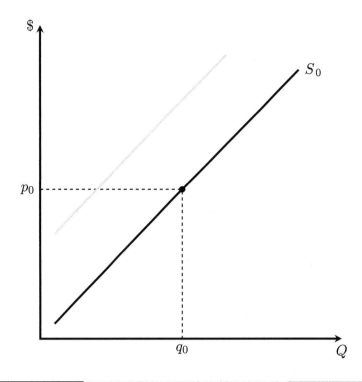

Notes for p.i.n.t.E. – Expectations about Future Prices

▶ **Expectations About Future Prices**
  ⋄ Example: Gasoline prices
  ⋄ Expected prices $\implies$ Supply

Wrap-up

▶ Buyers determine demand
  ◇ Relationship between price and quantity demanded
    • Inverse relationship

  ◇ Consumer surplus is the net benefit of consumption

▶ Sellers determined supply
  ◇ Relationship between price and quantity supplied
    • Positive relationship

  ◇ Producer surplus is the net benefit of production

▶ P.I.N.T.E. changes the relationship between price and quantity

Chapter 4

Equilibrium

Chapter 4: Market Equilibrium

Principles of Microeconomics

Prof. Greg Madonia

California State University, Chico

Outline

1. Markets

2. Equilibrium

3. Equilibrium and the Gains from Trade
   - Total Surplus
   - Non-equilibrium Outcomes

4. Changes in Equilibrium

What is a Market?

- Where buyers and sellers of a particular good or service interact
- The interaction of buyers and sellers determine:
    - The price at which a good is sold
    - The quantity that is sold
    - Which consumers get the good
    - Who produces the good or service

Initial Assumptions: Reminder

- Many buyers and sellers

- Buyers and sellers are small compared to the overall size of the market
    - No bargaining

Equilibrium

> **Definition: Equilibrium**
>
> The equilibrium concept in economics is where quantity demanded (q_d) is equal to the quantity supplied (q_s).
>
> $$q_e \equiv q_d = q_s$$

- **Equilibrium Price**: p_e (market clearing price)
  - Price at which $q_d = q_s$
- **Equilibrium Quantity**: q_e (market clearing quantity)
  - Occurs at the equilibrium price
- Visually, this is where supply and demand intersect...

Notes for Equilibrium

Equilibrium

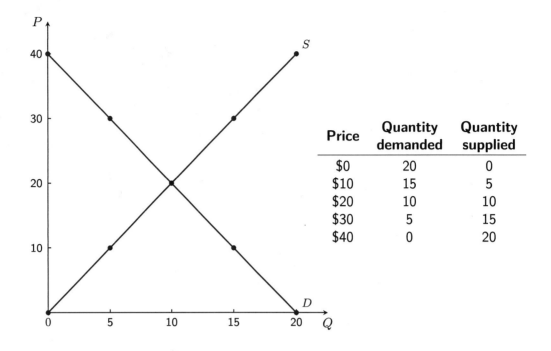

Notes for Equilibrium

Equilibrium: Results

▶ Equilibria are **stable**
  ◇ Gains from trade are maximized*
  ◇ No change until outside forces act on it
    •

▶ If a market is not in equilibrium, then _____ attempt to push the market to equilibrium
  ◇ Shortage or surplus of production
  ◇ Competition is the driving factor

Notes for Equilibrium: Results

Surplus (Excess Supply): $q_s > q_d$

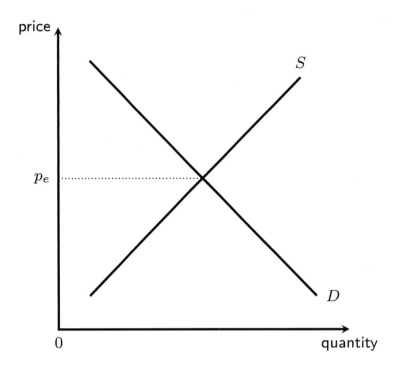

Notes for Surplus (Excess Supply): $q_s > q_d$

▶ Surplus
  ◇ $p > p_e$
  ◇ $\implies$
     • $\implies$
  ◇ _____
  ◇
     •

▶
  ◇
  ◇
  ◇
     • stops when

Shortage (Excess Demand): $q_s > q_d$

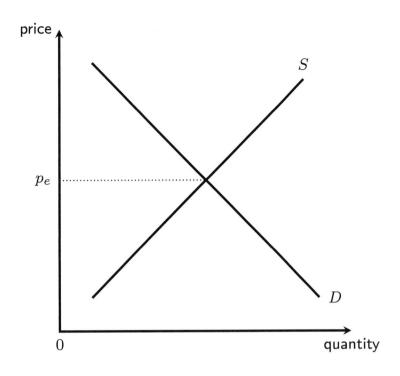

Notes for Shortage (Excess Demand): $q_s > q_d$

- Shortage
  - $p < p_e$
  - $\implies$
    - $\implies$
  - _____
-
  -
-
  -
  -
  -
    - stops when

Total Surplus

> **Definition: Total Surplus** (TS)
>
> Total surplus is the additional benefit that a unit of a good provides minus the cost of producing that additional unit.
> **For an individual quantity:**
>
> $$TS_i = MB_i - MC_i$$
>
> **For all quantities produced and consumed:**
>
> $$TS = TS_1 + TS_2 + TS_3 + \cdots$$
>
> which is sometimes referred to as the total total surplus

▶ Total surplus is the _____ of production and consumption

Notes for Total Surplus

Total Surplus - Visually

▶ Visually, total surplus is the area between the demand curve (MB) and the supply curve (MC) for all the units produced and consumed

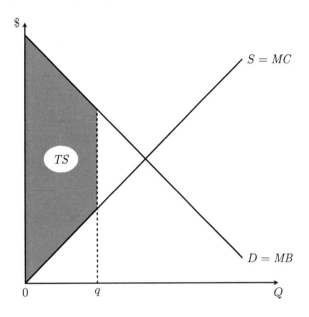

Total, Consumer, and Producer Surplus

▶ Since total surplus is the net benefit of production and consumption, we can relate it to both consumer and producer surpluses

$$TS_i = MB_i - MC_i$$
$$= MB_i - MC_i \underbrace{+ p - p}_{\text{adding 0}}$$
$$= MB_i - p + p - MC_i$$
$$= (MB_i - p) + (p - MC_i)$$
$$TS_i = CS_i + PS_i$$

Maximizing Total Surplus

- TS is a measure of well-being
- $\implies$ maximizing TS is how we make ourselves best-off
- How do we do this?
- Suppose we had access to an omniscient, omnibenevolent, and omnipotent being
    - Let's call this being the social planner
    - Give them the goal: maximize total surplus
    - Done by choosing the **right quantity**
        - Let's denote the right/optimal quantity as q^*

Notes for Maximizing Total Surplus

What is the "right" quantity (q^*)?

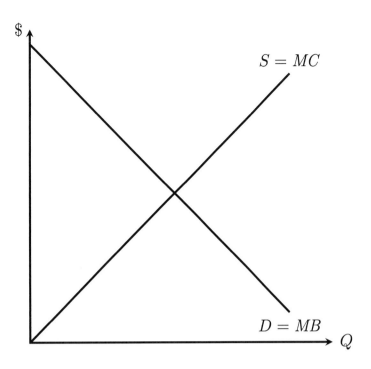

Notes for What is the "right" quantity (q^*)?

- At quantities less than q_e (e.g., __), _____ $\implies$ produce/consume ____

- At quantities greater than q_e (e.g., __), _____ $\implies$ produce/consume ____

- __ is the "right" quantity for the planner to choose
  ◇ q_e is the quantity where _____
  ◇ $q_e = $ __

How Is This "Right" Quantity Allocated?

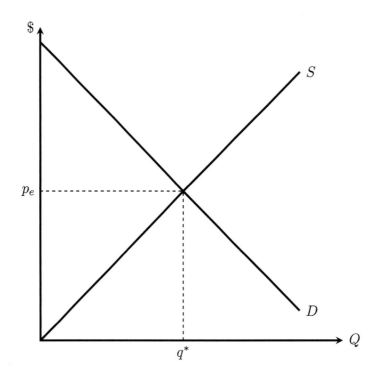

Notes for How Is This "Right" Quantity Allocated?

- ▶ Who gets the goods produced?
  - ◇ All consumers whose $MB \quad p$
  - ◇ _____ consumption

- ▶ Which units are produced?
  - ◇ All units whose $MC \quad p$
  - ◇ _____ production

What Happens When We Are Not at the "Right" Quantity?

- Still proceeding with our initial assumptions

- Equilibrium outcome produces the "right" quantity

- What are the consequences of a market that is not producing the "right" quantity?

Notes for What Happens When We Are Not at the "Right" Quantity?

Unexploited Gains

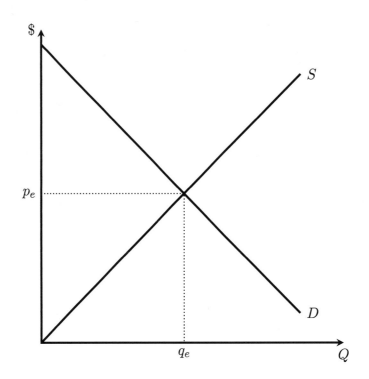

Notes for Unexploited Gains

- Suppose $p < p_e$
  - ⋄ ⟹
  - ⋄ also ⟹

- There are buyers who would pay at least p_e, but

- There are sellers who will sell more if

- Area _____ is the value of the

Wasted Resources

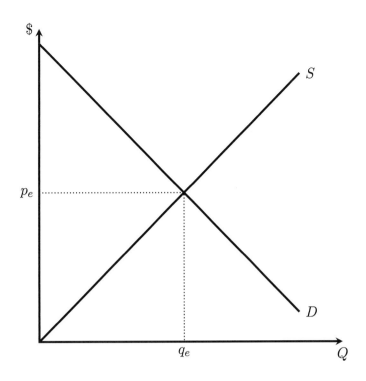

Notes for Wasted Resources

- $p > p_e$
  - ⋄ $\implies$
  - ⋄ also $\implies$

- There are units produced only because the price is

- The value of quantities above q_e is

- Area _____ is the value of the

The Market Maximizes the Gains from Trade

▶ Maximization rules

1. Units produced are purchased by the consumers with the highest willingness to pay

2. Units produced are sold by the sellers with the lowest costs

3. The quantity produced is the "right" quantity
   3.1 No unexploited gains from trade
   3.2 No wasted resources

▶ If a market meets these criteria then

Changes in Equilibrium

▶ Reminder: prices and quantities are stable at the equilibrium

▶ So, why do prices and quantities change?

▶ Law of Demand/Supply:
  ◇ ...holding other things constant
    • Changes in P.I.N.T.E.

Changes in Demand: Increase

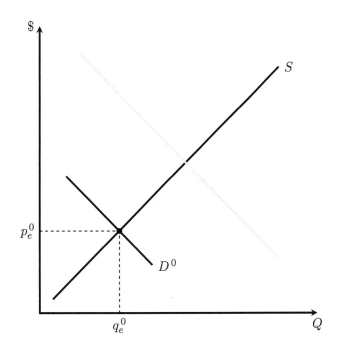

Notes for Changes in Demand: Increase

Demand Increases

- ⟹ _____ at p_e^0

- ⟹ p

- ⟹

- until
  - ◇
  - ◇

Changes in Demand: Decrease

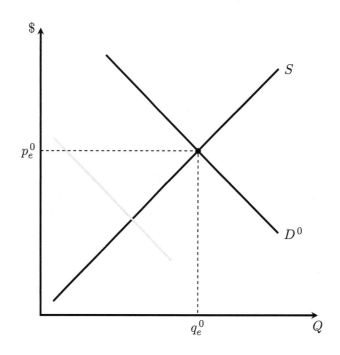

Notes for Changes in Demand: Decrease

Demand Decreases

▶ $\implies$ _____ at p_e^0

▶ $\implies p$

▶ $\implies$

▶ until
  ◇
  ◇

Changes in Supply: Increase

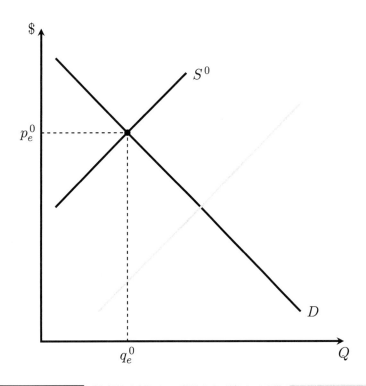

Notes for Changes in Supply: Increase

Supply Increases

- $\implies$ _____ at p_e^0

- $\implies p$

- $\implies$

- until
    - ◇
    - ◇

Changes in Supply: Decrease

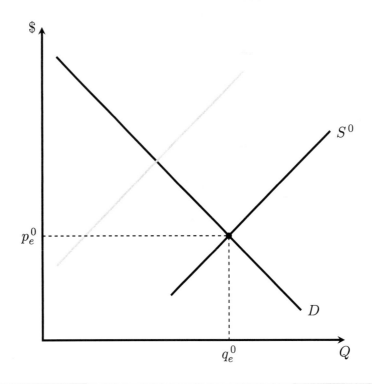

Notes for Changes in Supply: Decrease

Supply Decrease

- $\implies$ _____ at p_e^0

- $\implies p$

- $\implies$

- until
  - ◇
  - ◇

Supply and Demand Together

> **Definition: Law of Supply and Demand**
>
> The price of any good adjusts, if possible, to bring the quantity supplied and the quantity demanded for that good into balance

▶ In markets where prices **can** adjust, shortages and surpluses are temporary

  ◇ If prices cannot adjust, then shortages and surpluses can last indefinitely

3-step Recipe

1. Decide whether an event shifts the supply curve, the demand curve, both curves, or neither

2. If a shift exits, decide if the event increases or decreases the appropriate curve

3. Use the supply-and-demand graph
   3.1 Compare the initial equilibrium to the new equilibrium

   3.2 Note the change in equilibrium price and equilibrium quantity, if any

Example 1

Consider the market for donuts. Suppose a new scientific study is released that finds that consumption of donuts decreases cholesterol. Let's assume that supply is upward sloping and demand is downward sloping.

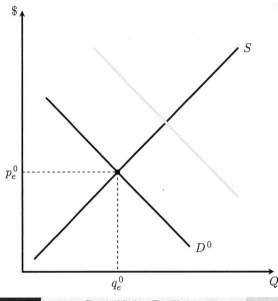

Notes for Example 1

- What variable changes and which curves are affected?
  - ◇
  - ◇

- Which direction does _____ shift?
  - ◇ _____

- What's the effect?
  - ◇ _____ $\implies q_e \quad p_e$

Example 2

Consider the market for ketchup. Suppose that the price of tomatoes rise. Let's also assume that supply is upward sloping and demand is downward sloping.

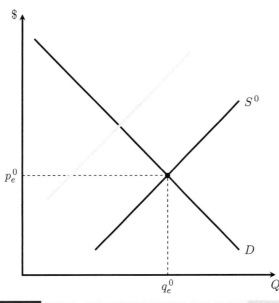

Notes for Example 2

- What variable changes and which curves are affected?
    - ◇
    - ◇

- Which direction does _____ shift?
    - ◇

- What's the effect?
    - ◇ $\implies q_e$ and p_e

Example 3

Consider the market for gasoline. Suppose that the price of gasoline is expected to increase tomorrow. Let's also assume that supply is upward sloping and demand is downward sloping.

▶ What variable changes and which curves are affected?
  ◇

▶ Which direction does _____ shift?
  ◇

▶ Which direction does _____ shift?
  ◇

▶ What's the effect?
  ◇ _____ _____

Notes for Example 3

Simultaneous Shifts

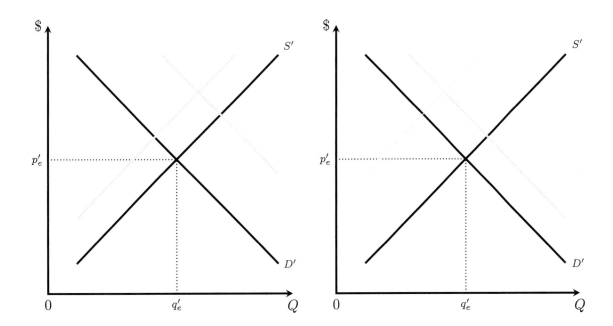

Notes for Simultaneous Shifts

Equilibrium Effects

Change	p_e	q_e	Change	p_e	q_e
D ↑	↑	↑	D ↑ S ↑		
D ↓	↓	↓	D ↑ S ↓		
S ↑	↓	↑	D ↓ S ↑		
S ↓	↑	↓	D ↓ S ↓		

▶ If upward sloping supply and downward sloping demand
  ◇ If one curve shifts
    • We know what direction both p_e and q_e move
  ◇ If both curve shifts:
    • Magnitude of shifts matter
    • We know what will happen to either p_e or q_e without further information
    • Need either graphical analysis or equations to find out the direction of change for both

Notes for Equilibrium Effects

Shifts vs. Movement Along

▶ Shift $\iff$ change in supply/demand

▶ Movement along $\iff$ change in quantiy supplied/quantity demanded

▶ One last time

  ◇ A change in the price of a good _____ the demand or supply for that good.

   • Movement along the relevent curve

Chapter 5

Elasticity

Chapter 5: Elasticity

Principles of Microeconomics

Prof. Greg Madonia

California State University, Chico

Outline

1. Elasticity of Demand (E_d)
   - Determinants of E_d

2. Other Demand Elasticities
   - Income Elasticity of Demand
   - Cross-price Elasticity of Demand

3. Price Elasticity of Supply

Elasticity of Demand

> **Definition: Elasticity**
>
> Elasticity is a measure of _____ one economic variable responds to changes in another economic variable

> **Definition: Price Elasticity of Demand** (ε_d)
>
> The responsiveness of the q_d of some good to changes in _____ ____
>
> $$E_d = \frac{\%\Delta q_d^x}{\%\Delta p^x}$$

- $E_d \neq m \equiv$ slope
- The more responsive a demand curve, the more _____ the demand curve

Some Initial Elasticity Calculation Examples

$$E_d = \frac{\%\Delta q_d^x}{\%\Delta p^x}$$

Example 1
- $\%\Delta q_d = -10$
- $\%\Delta p = 30$
- $E_d =$

Example 2
- $\%\Delta q_d =$
- $\%\Delta p = -5$
- $E_d = -2$

Elasticity of Demand (E_d)

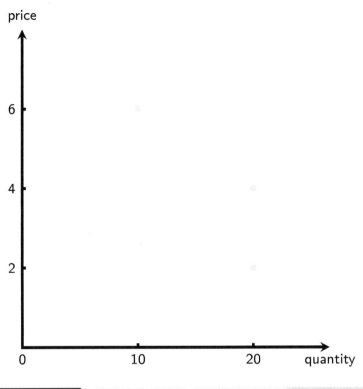

Notes for the Above Slide

- $A \longrightarrow B$
- $\%\Delta q_d = \frac{20-10}{10} \times 100 =$
- $\%\Delta p = \frac{4-6}{6} \times 100 =$
- $E_d =$
  ◇ Note: this is a unitless number
- What can we do with this number?
- $A \longrightarrow C$
- $\%\Delta q_d = \frac{20-10}{10} \times 100 =$
- $\%\Delta p = \frac{2-6}{6} \times 100 =$
- $E_d = \frac{100}{-66.7} =$
- Demand curve D is _____ than demand curve D' at the points considered

What Are the Determinants of E_d?

▶ **Availability of close substitutes**
  ◇ More close substitutes $\implies$ _____ demand

▶ **Time horizon**
  ◇ Longer time horizon $\implies$ more time to find _____ $\implies$ _____ demand

▶ **Definition of the market**
  ◇ More narrowly the market is defined $\implies$ more _____ $\implies$ _____ demand

What Are the Determinants of E_d? continued...

▶ **Necessities vs. Luxuries**
  ◇ Necessities (e.g., water) $\implies$ _____ $\implies$ _____ demand
  ◇ Luxuries (e.g., going out to dinner) $\implies$ _____ $\implies$ _____ demand

▶ **Share of Budget Devoted to the Good**
  ◇ Smaller the share $\implies$ _____

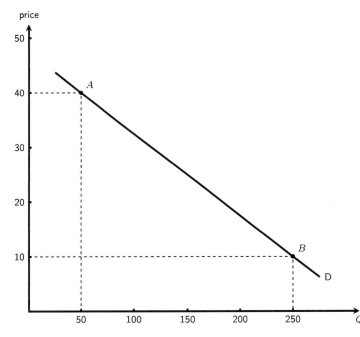

- $A \to B$
  - $E_d = -5.33$
  - relatively elastic
- $B \to A$
  - $E_d = -0.27$
  - relativey inelastic
- We would like a consistent measure of elasticity when we compare the same two points

Midpoint Method

Consider two points:

$$A = (q_1, p_1) = (50, \$40)$$
$$B = (q_2, p_2) = (250, \$10)$$

- Midpoint Method

$$E_d = \frac{\Delta q/\bar{q}}{\Delta p/\bar{p}} = \frac{\Delta q}{\bar{q}} \div \frac{\Delta p}{\bar{p}} = \frac{\Delta q}{\bar{q}} \times \frac{\bar{p}}{\Delta p}$$

- $\Delta q = q_2 - q_1 =$
- $\bar{q} = (q_2 + q_1)/2 =$
- $\Delta p = p_2 - p_1 =$
- $\bar{p} = (p_2 + p_1)/2 =$

$$E_d =$$

99

Categorization of Demand Elasticities

$$E_d = \frac{\%\Delta q_d}{\%\Delta p}$$

The numerical value of E_d allows us to categorize goods and services based on this value

- $E_d < -1$
    - Demand is _____
    - q_d responds _____ to a change in p

- $E_d = -1$
    - Demand is _____
    - q_d responds _____ to a change in p

- $0 \geq E_d > -1$
    - Demand is _____
    - q_d responds _____ to a change in p

Special Cases of E_d

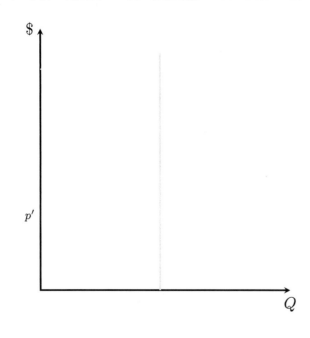

$$E_d = \frac{\%\Delta q_d}{\%\Delta p}$$

- $E_d = 0$
    - Demand is **perfectly inelastic**
    - q_d _____ to a change in p
    - Example:

Special Cases of E_d

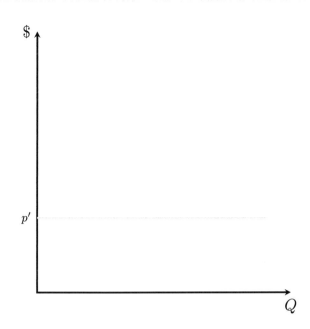

$$E_d = \frac{\%\Delta q_d}{\%\Delta p}$$

- $\varepsilon_d \approx -\infty$
  ◇ Demand is **perfectly elastic**
  ◇ q_d _____ to a change in p
  ◇ Example:

Rule of Thumb

▶ Suppose that there is the same change in price for two curves

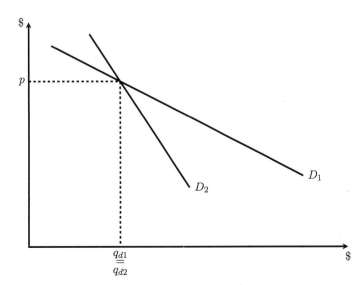

▶ **Rule**: If two straight line demand curves intersect, the flatter curve is

Price Elasticity of Demand and a Firm's Revenues

▶ TR is the amount paid by buyers and received by sellers for a good or service

$$TR = p \times q$$

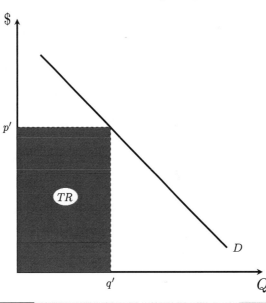

What Happens to TR When Price Changes?

Case 1: $0 \geq E_d > -1$

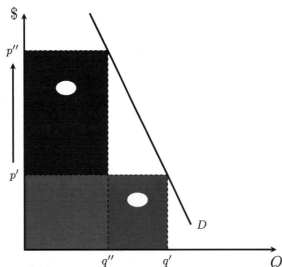

- area(A)   area(B)
- When $0 \geq E_d > -1$:
  ◇ If p

What Happens to TR When Price Changes?

Case 2: $E_d < -1$

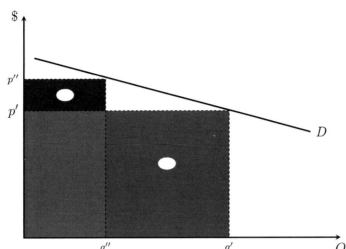

- area(A)   area(B)
- When $E_d < -1$:
  ◇ If p
- **Case 3:** $E_d = -1 : p \uparrow \implies TR\ -$, and vice-versa

Notes for What Happens to TR When Price Changes?

Income Elasticity of Demand (E_y)

- How much quantity demanded changes after a change in income (y), all else equal:
$$E_y = \frac{\%\Delta q_d}{\%\Delta \text{Income}} = \frac{\%\Delta q_d}{\%\Delta y}$$

- Can use the midpoint method to calculate
$$E_y = \frac{\Delta q_d / \bar{q}_d}{\Delta y / \bar{y}} = \frac{(q_{d2} - q_{d1})/[(q_{d2} + q_{d1})/2]}{(y_2 - y_1)/[(y_2 + y_1)/2]} = \frac{\Delta q_d}{\bar{q}_d} \times \frac{\bar{y}}{\Delta y}$$

- _____

  ◊ Law of demand $\implies E_d$ was never positive
  ◊ Be consistent with (q_{d1}, y_1) and (q_{d2}, y_2)

Notes for Income Elasticity of Demand (E_y)

Categorizing Goods Based on $E_y \left(= \frac{\%\Delta q_d}{\%\Delta y}\right)$

The sign matters because it allows us to categorize goods
- $E_y \geq 0$
  - Income and quantity demanded move in the _____
    - These are _____
  - $1 \geq E_y \geq 0$
    - Quantity demanded changes less than proportionally to a change in income
    - These are _____
    - Example:
  - $E_y > 1$
    - Quantity demanded changes more than proportionally to a change in income
    - These are _____
    - Example:
- $E_y < 0$
  - Income and quantity demanded move in the _____
    - These are _____

Notes for Categorizing Goods Based on $E_y \left(= \frac{\%\Delta q_d}{\%\Delta y}\right)$

Cross-price Elasticity of Demand ($E_{a,b}$)

- How much does the quantity demanded of some good, a, change when the price of *another* good, b, changes?

$$E_{a,b} = \frac{\%\Delta q_d^a}{\%\Delta p^b}$$

- Can use the midpoint method to calculate

$$E_{a,b} = \frac{\Delta q_d^a / \overline{q}_d^a}{\Delta p^b / \overline{p}^b} = \frac{(q_{d2}^a - q_{d1}^a)/[(q_{d2}^a + q_{d1}^a)/2]}{(p_2^b - p_1^b)/[(p_2^b + p_1^b)/2]} = \frac{\Delta q_d^a}{\overline{q}_d^a} \times \frac{\overline{p}^b}{\Delta p^b}$$

- Just like E_y, _____
  ◇ Be consistent with (q_{d1}^a, p_1^b) and (q_{d2}^a, p_2^b)

Notes for Cross-price Elasticity of Demand ($E_{a,b}$)

Categorizing Goods Based on $E_{a,b}$

$$E_{a,b} = \frac{\%\Delta q_d^a}{\%\Delta p^b}$$

- $E_{a,b} > 0$
    - Price of the other good and the quantity demanded of the good in question move in _____
        - These goods are _____

- $E_{a,b} < 0$
    - Price of the other good and the quantity demanded of the good in question move in _____
        - These goods are _____

- $E_{a,b} = 0$
    - These goods are _____

Notes for Categorizing Goods Based on $E_{a,b}$

Price Elasticity of Supply (E_s)

> **Definition: Elasticity of Supply**
>
> The responsiveness of quantity supplied (q_s) to changes in its own price
> $$E_s = \frac{\%\Delta q_s^x}{\%\Delta p^x}$$

▶ This is a measure of how sellers respond to changes in a goods price

  ◇ Price elasticity of supply depends on the flexibility of sellers to change the amount of the good they produce

Determinants of Price Elasticity of Supply

▶ **How Quickly Per-unit Costs Increase**
  ◇ The faster that per-unit cost of production increases, the more _____ is supply

▶ **Geography of the market**
  ◇ Local supply is more _____ than global supply

▶ **Time**
  ◇ Supply is more _____ in the long-run

▶ **Fixed inputs**
  ◇ Example: champagne
  ◇ # of fixed inputs $\implies E_s$

Midpoint Method

▶ Midpoint method for ε_s for two points: (q_1, p_1) and (q_2, p_2)

$$E_s = \frac{\Delta q_s / \overline{q}_s}{\Delta p / \overline{p}}$$
$$= \frac{(q_2 - q_1)/[(q_2 + q_1)/2]}{(p_2 - p_1)/[(p_2 + p_1)/2]} = \frac{\Delta q_s}{\overline{q}_s} \times \frac{\overline{p}}{\Delta p}$$

▶ Supply is *not* downward-sloping $\Longrightarrow$
▶ Categorizing based on the value of E_s:
  ⋄ $E_s > 1$:
  ⋄ $E_s = 1$:
  ⋄ $0 \leq E_s < 1$:

Special Cases of E_s

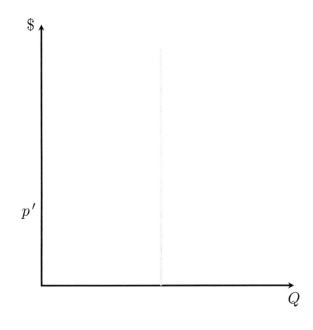

$$E_s = \frac{\% \Delta q_s}{\% \Delta p}$$

▶ $E_s = 0$
  ⋄ Supply is **perfectly inelastic**
  ⋄ q_s _____ to a change in p
  ⋄ Example:

Special Cases of E_s

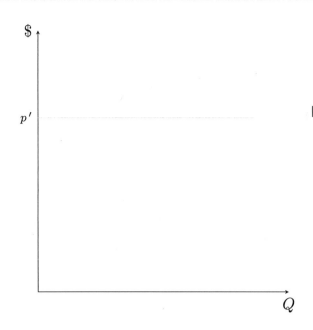

$$E_s = \frac{\%\Delta q_s}{\%\Delta p}$$

▶ $\varepsilon_s \approx \infty$
  ◇ Supply is **perfectly elastic**
  ◇ q_s _____ to a change in p
  ◇ Example:

Supply Rule of Thumb

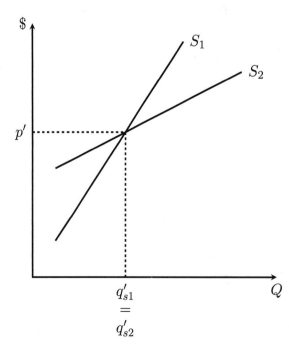

▶ Just like demand, the flatter curve is _____

Elasticities of Supply on the Same Supply Curve

Generally, a supply curve has different elasticities on the same curve
- ▶ Points with low price and low quantity supplied
  - ◇ elastic supply
  - ◇ capacity for production is not being utilized
- ▶ Points with high price and high quantity supplied
  - ◇ inelastic supply
  - ◇ even as price increases, firms find it hard to increase quantity supplied due to capacity constraints

Chapter 6

Taxes and Subsidies

Chapter 6: Taxes and Subsidies
Principles of Microeconomics

Prof. Greg Madonia

California State University, Chico

Outline

1. Taxes
   - The Impact of a Tax on Market Outcomes
   - Elasticity and the Tax Burden
   - Tax Revenue and Economic Efficiency

2. Subsidies
   - Subsidy Incidence

Taxes

> **Definition: Commodity Taxes**
>
> A **commodity tax** is a tax placed on goods, such as gasoline, beer, clothes, etc...

▶ Same results if we place a tax on anything that has "units" attached to it (for example, haircuts, streaming services, etc...)

▶ Assumptions:
  1. Taxes are "per unit"
  2. Taxes are constant

> **Definition: Tax Incidence**
>
> The **tax incidence** is the manner in which the burden of a tax is _____ among participants in the market

▶ Tax incidence is what economists care about
  ◇ Not necessarily who the tax is collected from

$$p_b : \text{Price that buyers pay}$$
$$p_s : \text{Price that sellers receive}$$

▶ Without taxes (or other market interventions):

  ◇ Tax incidence will be measured by the difference between p_b/p_s and p_e (more later)

A Tax Shifts Demand or Supply

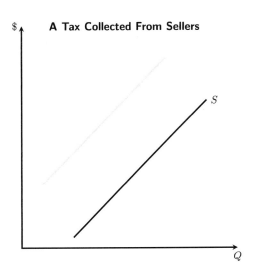
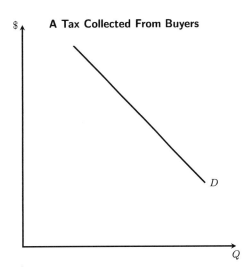

- A tax collected from sellers _____ the supply curve _____ _____ at all quantities
- A tax collected from buyers _____ the demand curve _____ _____ at all quantities

Notes for A Tax Shifts Demand or Supply

Equilibrium Prior to a Tax

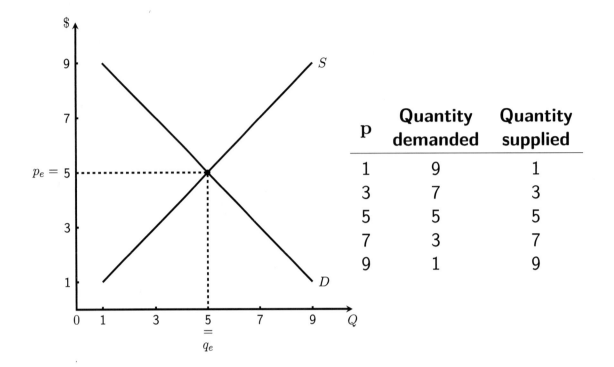

Notes for Equilibrium Prior to a Tax

A $4 Tax on Sellers

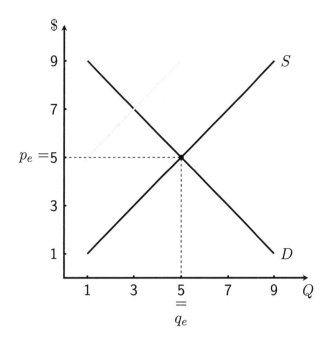

Notes for A $4 Tax on Sellers

P	Quantity demanded	Quantity supplied	Quantity supplied with tax
1	9	1	
3	7	3	
5	5	5	
7	3	7	
9	1	9	

▶
▶ New equilibrium
  ◇
    • Size of the market is
  ◇
  ◇

▶ Instead, what if we collect the same tax from buyers...?

A $4 Tax on Buyers

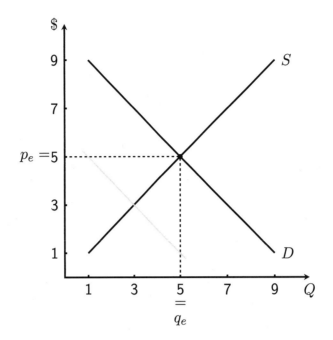

Notes for A $4 Tax on Buyers

P	Quantity demanded	Quantity supplied	Quantity demanded with tax
1	9	1	
3	7	3	
5	5	5	
7	3	7	
9	1	9	

▶

▶ New equilibrium
  ◇
   • Size of the market is
  ◇
  ◇

▶ _____ result as if we had collected the tax from sellers

The Tax Wedge

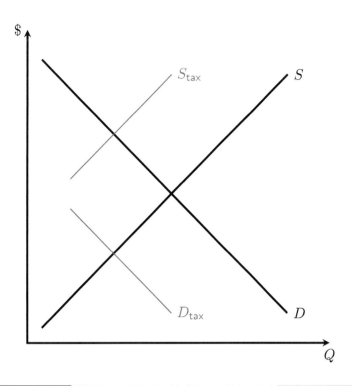

Notes for The Tax Wedge

- A tax on sellers produces the _____ as a tax on buyers

- A _____ between the prices buyers pay (p_b) and the prices sellers receive (p_s)

- tax =

Calculating the Tax Burden

- Economists care about the tax burden
- Tax burden is a per unit measure
- Burden is the difference between tax outcome and non-tax outcome

$$\text{burden on buyers} =$$
$$\text{burden on sellers} =$$

- Note:

$$\text{tax} = p_b - p_s$$
$$= p_b - p_s \underbrace{+ p_e - p_e}_{\text{adding 0}}$$
$$= (p_b - p_e) + (p_e - p_s)$$
$$\text{tax} =$$

Is the Burden Split Evenly Between Buyers and Sellers?

- We now know that buyers and sellers share the burden of a tax — regardless of who the tax is collected from
  ◇ Caveat to that in a minute...

- This prompts the question: is the burden split evenly?
  ◇ How the burden is split depends on the _____ and _____
  ◇ Short answer:

Elasticity and Tax Incidence

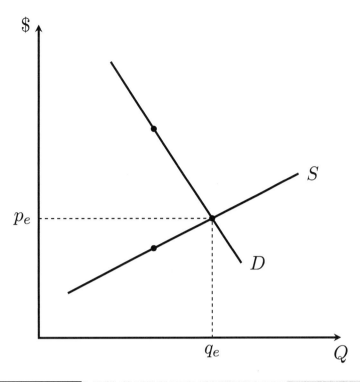

Notes for Elasticity and Tax Incidence

Relatively elastic supply and relatively inelastic demand

- Sellers: relatively _____ to respond to changes in price
  - ⟹

- Buyers: relatively _____ to respond to changes in price
  - ⟹

- Conclusion: Burden on sellers _____ than the burden on buyers

Elasticity and Tax Incidence

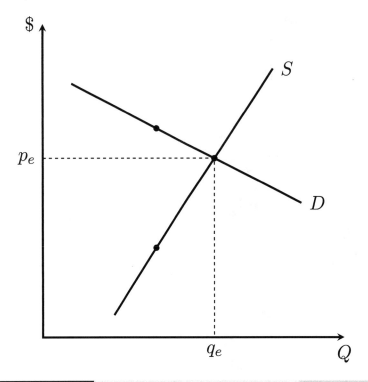

Notes for Elasticity and Tax Incidence

Relatively inelastic supply and relatively elastic demand
- Sellers: relatively _____ to respond to changes in price
  - $\implies$
- Buyers: relatively _____ to respond to changes in price
  - $\implies$
- Conclusion: Burden on sellers _____ than the burden on buyers

Caveat to Sharing the Burden

▶ Caveat: Perfectly inelastic supply or demand

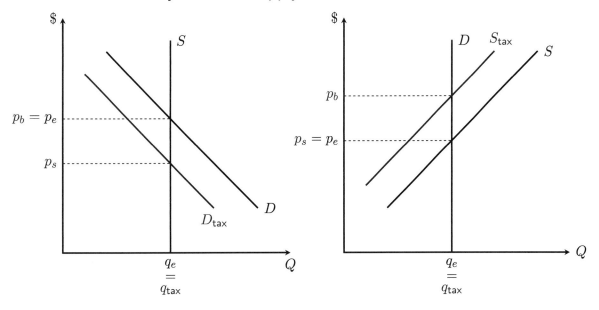

Who's Bearing the Majority of the Burden?

Different taxes to think about and who the majority of the burden falls on (that is, consumers or producers)

▶ Tax on yachts

▶ Tax on food

▶ Tax on labor

▶ Tax on gasoline

123

Tax Burden Wrap-Up

▶ Falls more heavily on the side of the market that is _____

▶ Small elasticity of demand
  ◇ Buyers do not have good alternatives to consuming the good

▶ Small elasticity of supply
  ◇ Sellers do not have a good alternative to producing the good

▶ _____ determine who bears the majority of the burden of the tax

Preview of the Results

▶ No taxes: consumer, producer, and total surpluses are _____

▶ With a tax: consumer, producer, and total surpluses _____
  ◇ But tax revenues are raised...
  ◇ The losses in the surpluses _____ than the gains of tax revenue
  ◇ Deadweight loss
    • Efficiency losses

Measuring the Gains of a Tax

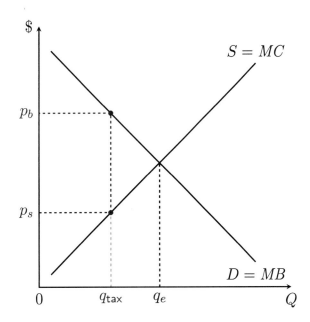

Notes for Measuring the Gains of a Tax

- Tax revenue (GR)

- GR = quantity sold × size of the tax
  - quantity sold
  - size of the tax

- Tax revenue is the public benefit of the tax
  - Can be included in total surplus

Deadweight Loss

Losses of Surplus to Buyers and Sellers from a Tax
- ▶ Losses exceed the revenue raised by a government
  - ◇ Taxes lead to a net loss
  - ◇ Assume: the supply curve (MC) captures all costs and the demand curve (MB) captures all benefits
- ▶ What happens to the rest?

> **Definition: Deadweight Loss**
>
> Reduction in _____ that results from any market distortion, such as a tax

- ▶ Taxes distort incentives
  - ◇ Markets allocate resources inefficiently

Notes for Deadweight Loss

Visualizing Surplus, Tax Revenue, and Deadweight Loss

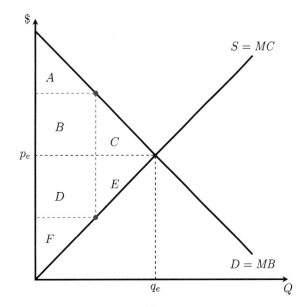

Notes for Visualizing Surplus, Tax Revenue, and Deadweight Loss

Without tax...
1. $CS =$
2. $PS =$
3. $TS =$
4. $GR =$
5. $DWL =$

With tax...
1. $CS =$
2. $PS =$
3. $TS =$
4. $GR =$
5. $DWL =$

Deadweight Loss and the Grains From Trade

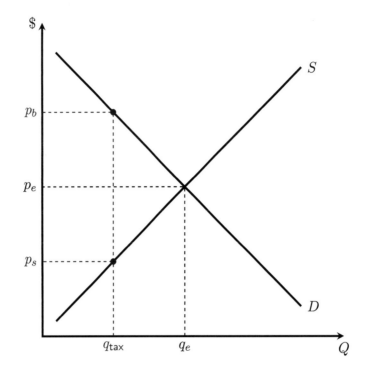

Notes for Deadweight Loss and the Grains From Trade

▶ Taxes cause
  ◇ Prevents buyers and sellers from realizing some of the gains from trade

▶ The gains from trade
  ◇ Difference between buyers' _____ and sellers' _____

▶ Once the tax is imposed
  ◇ Some trades _____ are no longer made
    •

Measuring Deadweight Loss of a Tax

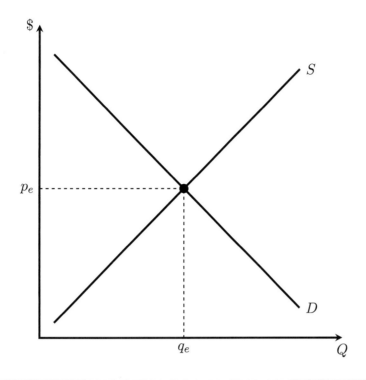

Notes for Measuring Deadweight Loss of a Tax

- Taxes reduced the size of the market: $q_e \to q_{\text{tax}}$

- Value of the lost quantities:

- Cost of the lost quantities:

- Total loss:
$$DWL =$$

Elasticity, Tax Size, and Deadweight Loss

- So far
  - Relative elasticities determine relative burden
  - Taxes reduce the size of the market
  - Taxes cause deadweight loss

- How do the elasticities of supply and demand determine the efficiency impact of a tax?

Holding Both Demand and the Size of the Tax Constant...

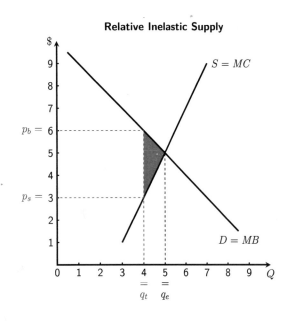 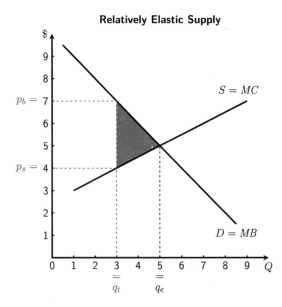

Deadweight loss (■) _____ with the price elasticity of supply

Holding Both Supply and the Size of the Tax Constant...

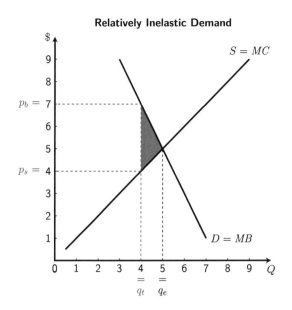
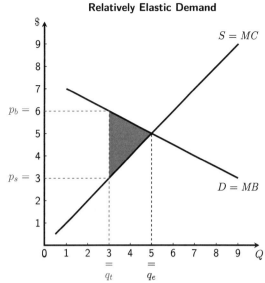

Deadweight loss (■) _____ with the price elasticity of demand

All Else Equal, as the Size of a Tax Increases...

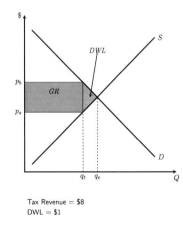
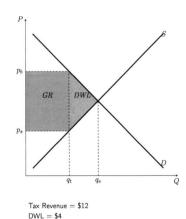
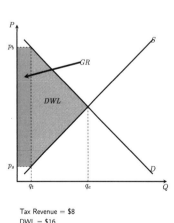

Tax Revenue = $8   Tax Revenue = $12   Tax Revenue = $8
DWL = $1   DWL = $4   DWL = $16

▶ Going from left to right, as the size of the tax $(p_b - p_s)$ increases...
  ◇ Tax revenue (GR) initially _____ and then _____
  ◇ Deadweight loss (DWL) _____ and then _____

Tax Wrap-Up

▶ Taxes increase prices for buyers and lower prices for sellers

▶ Taxes reduce consumer and producer surpluses but raise tax revenue
  ◇ Revenue raise is less than the loss in surplus: deadweight loss

▶ Price elasticities of supply and demand determine
  ◇ Relative tax burdens
  ◇ Amount of deadweight loss generated

Notes

Subsidies

> **Definition: Subsidy**
>
> A subsidy is a per-unit payment from the government to either consumers or producers for consuming or producing a good/service, respectively

- Negative/reverse tax

- Examples:
    - Flu shots
    - Agricultural production
    - Education
    - Wages for post-incarceration felons

Subsidy-Tax Similarities

- Since subsides are a "negative tax" $\implies$ analogous results

1. Results are the same regardless of whether consumers or producers receive the subsidy

2. Relative price elasticities of supply and demand determine which side of the market gets the most benefit

3. Subsidies create deadweight loss*

Consumers Receive the Subsidy

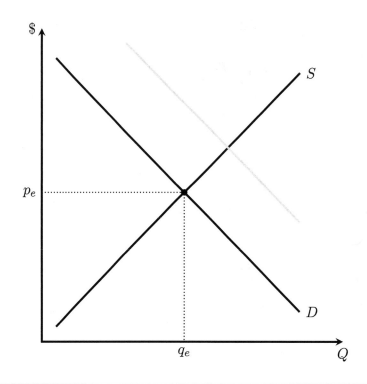

Notes for Consumers Receive the Subsidy

- Customers get _____ for every unit they purchase
  - Additional value is the size of the subsidy
  - Demand

- New equilibrium outcome
  -
  -
  -

Producers Receive the Subsidy

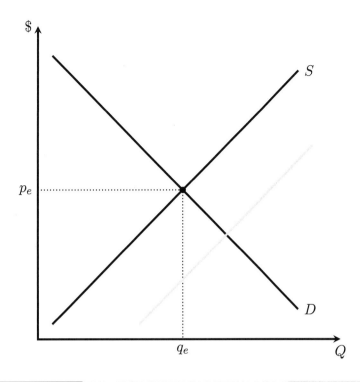

Notes for Producers Receive the Subsidy

- Producer's net costs for every unit they produce
  - Reduction in cost is the size of the subsidy
  - Supply
- New equilibrium outcome
  - ◇
  - ◇
  - ◇
- _____ outcome as when consumers receive the subsidy

Subsidy Wedge

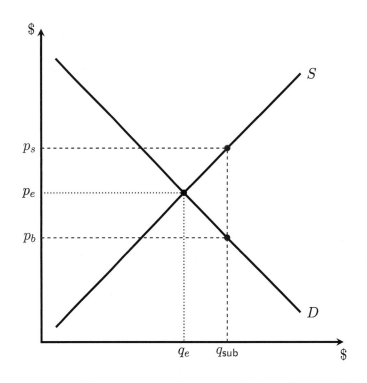

Notes for Subsidy Wedge

- Does not matter who receives the subsidy

- Can represent the subsidy outcome with a

- subsidy wedge =

- Subsidies require

Subsidies and Government Expenditure

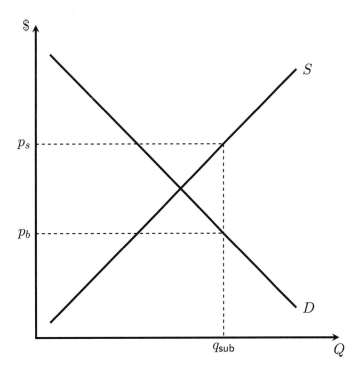

Notes for Subsidies and Government Expenditure

▶ Government pays the subsidy for each unit produced and consumed
  ◇ "price" =
  ◇ quantity =

▶ Government expenditure

  =

▶ Ultimately, a ___ to the taxpayers
  ◇

Subsidies and Deadweight Loss

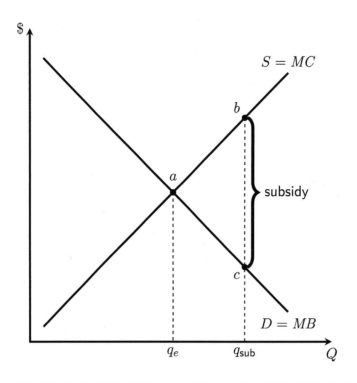

Notes for Subsidies and Deadweight Loss

- q_e is the last quantity where

- Consider
    - ◇ _____

- Subsides create

- Size of the
    - ◇

=

Definition: Subsidy Incidence

The **subsidy incidence** is the manner in which the benefit of a subsidy is ____ among participants in the market

- Subsidy incidence is a per unit measure
- Benefit is the difference between subsidy outcome and non-subsidy outcome

$$\text{benefit to buyers} =$$
$$\text{burden on sellers} =$$

- Note:
$$\text{subsidy} = p_s - p_b$$
$$= p_s - p_b \underbrace{+ p_e - p_e}_{\text{adding 0}}$$
$$= (p_s - p_e) + (p_e - p_b)$$
$$\text{subsidy} =$$

Notes

Elasticity and Subsidy Incidence

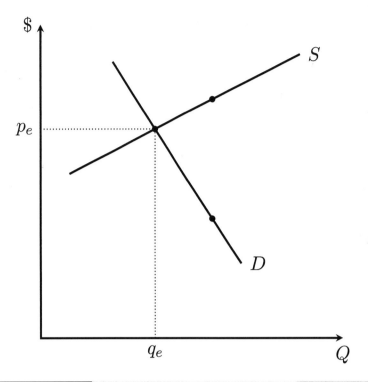

Notes for Elasticity and Subsidy Incidence

Relatively elastic supply and relatively inelastic demand
- Sellers: relatively _____ to respond to changes in price
  - ⟹
- Buyers: relatively _____ to respond to changes in price
  - ⟹
- Conclusion: Benefit to buyers _____ than the benefit to sellers

Elasticity and Subsidy Incidence

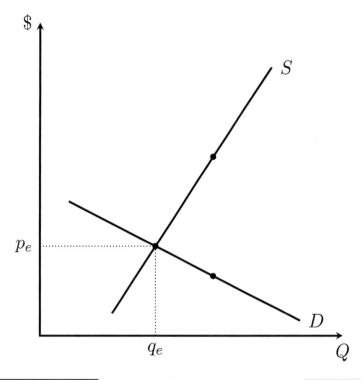

Notes for Elasticity and Subsidy Incidence

Relatively inelastic supply and relatively elastic demand
- Sellers: relatively _____ to respond to changes in price
  ◇ ⟹
- Buyers: relatively _____ to respond to changes in price
  ◇ ⟹
- Conclusion: Benefit to sellers _____ than the benefit to buyers

Who's Getting the Majority of the Benefit?

Who gets the majority of the benefit? Consumers or producers?

- Subsidy on almonds (via water use)
- Flu shots
- Education
- Wages for post-incarceration felons
- Housing
- Food
- Green energy

Subsidies Wrap-Up

- Subsidies decrease prices for buyers and increase prices for sellers

- Subsidies increase the quantity consumed in the market
    - Creates deadweight loss if the market quantity was the "right" quantity

- Price elasticties of supply and demand determine
    - Relative subsidy benefits

Chapter 8

Price Controls

Chapter 8: Price Controls
Principles of Microeconomics

Prof. Greg Madonia

California State University, Chico

Outline

1. Price Controls

2. Price Ceilings

3. Price Floors

Price Controls

> **Definition: Price Control**
>
> A price control is a _____ on the price at which a good can be sold

- Examples:
- Legal maximum: price ceiling
- Legal minimum: price floor
- Distorts market incentives
- Links and de-links markets in ways that can cause inefficiency losses

Arguments for Price Controls

- Price maximums (ceilings)
    - Price gauging
    - Strain on lower income households
- Price minimums (floors)
    - Over-consumption of "bad stuff"
    - Help lower-income workers

Price Ceiling

> **Definition: Price Ceiling**
>
> A price ceiling is a legal maximum on the price at which a good can be sold

- A price control can either matter (binding) or not (non-binding)
- A binding price ceiling can lead to five important consequences:
    1. Shortages
    2. Reductions in product quality
    3. Wasteful queuing and search costs
    4. Deadweight loss
    5. Mis-allocated resources

Notes for Price Ceiling

Binding and Non-binding Price Ceilings

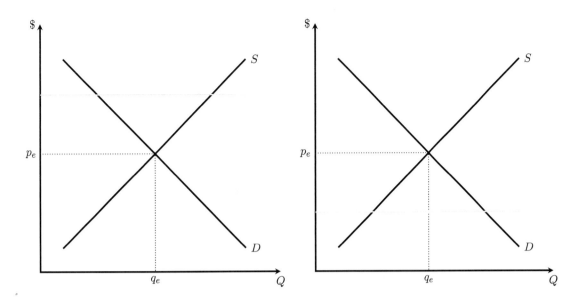

- If p_c $p_e \implies q_s$ $q_d \implies p_c$ is
- If p_c $p_e \implies q_s$ $q_d \implies p_c$ is

Notes for Binding and Non-binding Price Ceilings

Consequence 1: Shortages

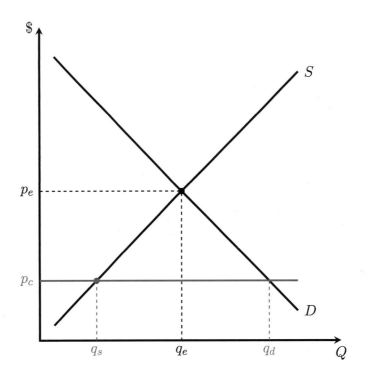

Notes for Consequence 1: Shortages

When a price ceiling is binding

- $q_s \neq q_d$

- $q_s < q_d$
  - $\diamond \implies$

- There are buyers who want to buy the good at the price ceiling and

- There are buyers who would pay the equilibrium price and

Consequence 2: Reductions in Quality

- Shortage
  - Partially the result of the supply curve being upward sloping

- Producers _____ to satiate demand
  - Can take the form of worse service

- Producers can also _____ of the products
  -

Notes for Consequence 2: Reductions in Quality

Consequence 3: Waiting in Line and Bribes

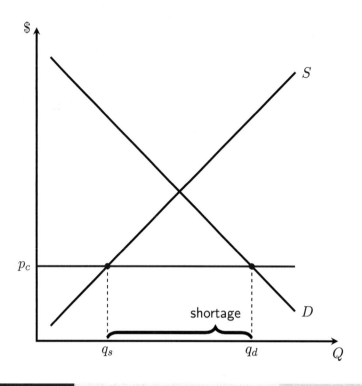

Notes for Consequence 3: Waiting in Line and Bribes

▶ At the binding price ceiling, there are some consumers willing to pay more

▶ Consumers can pay a
  ◇ Pay, in opportunity costs, up to the
  ◇ Value goes to

▶ Consumers can bribe the supplier
  ◇ Pay up to the
  ◇ Value goes to

Consequence 4: Deadweight Loss

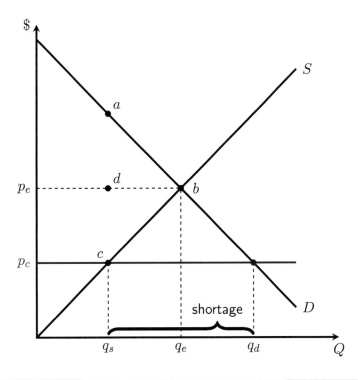

Notes for Consequence 4: Deadweight Loss

- Consumer surplus
- Producer surplus
- Some trades where MB MC
  - ◇
    - •
  - ◇ Consumers lose
  - ◇ Producers lose
- _____ transferred from producers to consumers
- Assumption: highest value uses get the goods
  - ◇ Minimizes deadweight loss

Consequence 5: Mis-allocated Resources

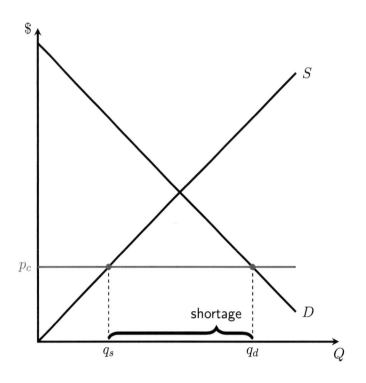

Notes for Consequence 5: Mis-allocated Resources

- In a free market, all consumers whose _____ get the good

- Price ceiling
  ◦ Shortages
  ◦ _____ consumers whose $MB > p$ get the good

- Even worse, no guarantee that the consumers with the _____ get the good
  ◦

- Prices cannot increase $\Longrightarrow$

Spillovers

- Price ceilings $\implies$ shortages

- Shortages in one market can spill over into other markets

- Example
  - Energy crisis in the 1970s was made worse due to lack of drilling equipment – caused by price controls in the steel market

Price Floors

Definition: Price Floor

A price floor is a legal minimum on the price at which a good can be sold

- A price floor can either matter (binding) or not (non-binding)
- A binding price floor can lead to four important consequences:
  1. Surpluses
  2. Deadweight loss
  3. Wasteful increases in product quality
  4. Mis-allocated resources

Binding and Non-binding Price Floors

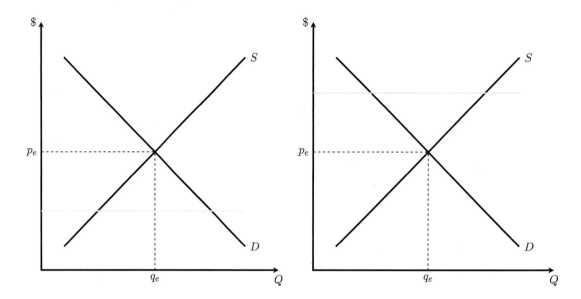

- If p_f $p_e \implies q_s$ $q_d \implies p_f$ is
- If p_f $p_e \implies q_s$ $q_d \implies p_f$ is

Notes for Binding and Non-binding Price Floors

Consequence 2: Deadweight Loss

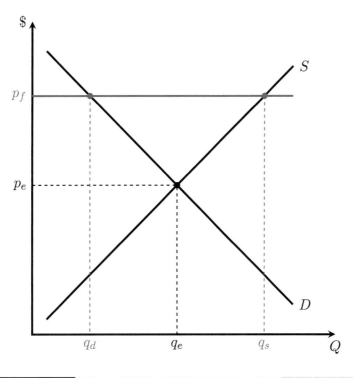

Notes for Consequence 2: Deadweight Loss

When a price floor is binding

- $q_s \neq q_d$
- $q_s > q_d$
  - ⟹

- There are sellers who want to sell their goods at the price floor and

- There are sellers who would sell at the equilibrium price and

- Labor market surpluses:

Consequence 2: Deadweight Loss

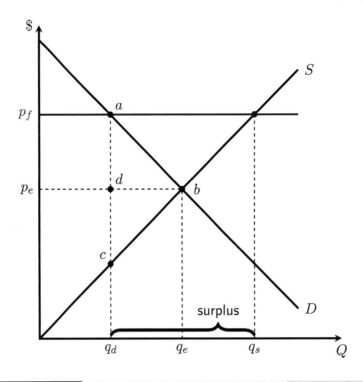

Notes for Consequence 2: Deadweight Loss

- Consumer surplus
- Producer surplus
- Some trades where MB ____ MC
  - ◇
    - •
  - ◇ Consumers lose
  - ◇ Producers lose
- _____ transferred from consumers to producers
- Assumption: lowest cost producers produce the good
  - ◇ Minimizes deadweight loss

Consequence 3: Wasteful Increases in Quality

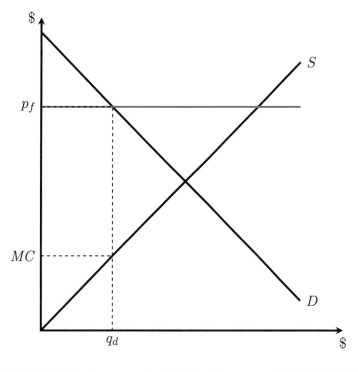

Notes for Consequence 3: Wasteful Increases in Quality

- ▶ Producers cannot lower prices to compete with one another
- ▶ Producers must find other ways to attract buyers
  - ◇
  - ◇ Example:

Consequence 4: Mis-allocated Resources

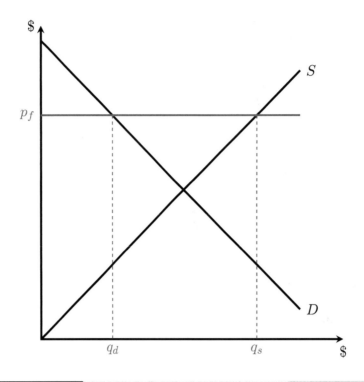

Notes for Consequence 4: Mis-allocated Resources

- In a free market, only the producers with the lowest costs are in the market

- Price floors
  - ⋄ ⟹

- No guarantee that the _____ producers survive

- Since prices are artificially high ⟹

Chapter Wrap-up

▶ Price controls can either put a legal maximum or a legal minimum on prices

▶ Price controls do not necessarily matter

▶ Binding price controls
  ◇ Create shortages or surpluses
  ◇ Generate deadweight loss
  ◇ Mis-allocate resources

Chapter 10
Externalities

Chapter 10: Externalities
Principles of Microeconomics

Prof. Greg Madonia

California State University, Chico

Outline

1. Introduction

2. Externalities

3. Externalities & Market Outcomes
   - Negative Externalities
   - Positive Externalities

4. Solutions to the Externality Problem
   - Corrective Taxes and Subsidies
   - Private Solutions: The Coase Theorem

An Example: Electricity Production

- Energy is a "necessary" component of modern life
- Do we produce the "right" amount of electricity?
- Every time a unit of electricity is produced
  - The consumer gets the benefit
  - The producer incurs the cost of production
  - Bystanders get polluted on
    - This is a cost

An Example: Electricity Production

- We have not considered this additional cost to bystanders thus far
- Whenever there are significant spillover costs, or benefits, on bystanders $\implies$ **market failure**
- The price signal produced by the market is no longer correct
  - Electricity prices are "too low"

Externalities

> **Definition: Externality**
>
> The _____ impact of one person's actions on the well-being of a _____

- The presence of an externality can lead to a
- Negative externality
    - Impact on the bystander is adverse
    - _____ fails to take into account the externality's additional cost
- Positive externality
    - Impact on the bystander is beneficial
    - _____ fails to take into account the externality's additional benefit

Preview of the Results

Market Equilibrium Under the Presence of an Externality
- Inefficient allocation of resources
- Buyers and sellers neglect the external effects of their actions when deciding how much to demand or supply
- Fails to maximize the total benefit to society as a whole

Government
- Has the potential to protect the interests of bystanders (those whom the externality is imposed on)

Welfare Economics: A Recap

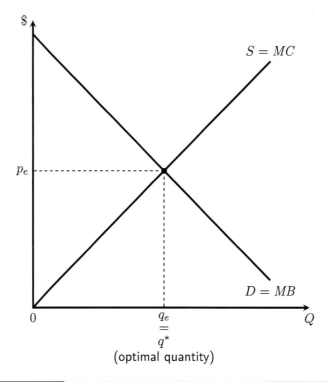

Notes for Welfare Economics: A Recap

- ▶ Demand curve: value to consumers
- ▶ Supply curve: cost to suppliers
- ▶ Equilibrium quantity and price
  - ◇ Efficient
  - ◇ Only quantities where the marginal benefit is greater than the marginal cost are produced and consumed
  - ◇ Maximize sum of producer and consumer surplus
- ▶ Without the presence of externalities, the equilibrium quantity (q_e) is the optimal/efficient quantity (q^*)

Efficiency Definitions

Definition: Social Surplus

Consumer surplus plus producer surplus

Definition: Efficient Equilibrium

The price and quantity that maximize social surplus

Definition: Optimal (Efficient) Quantity (q^*)

The quantity that maximizes social surplus

Negative Externalities

- Additional cost to society of producing a good
  - $\implies$ _____ of production is larger than the cost to the producers of the good
  - Examples:

- Marginal Private Cost (MPC)
  - The additional cost of producing one more unit for
  - Without externalities

- Marginal External Cost (MEC)
  - The additional cost of producing one more unit for
  - With externalities

Marginal Social Cost

▶ Marginal Social Cost (MSC)
  ◇ Private costs to the producers ____ the costs to the bystanders affected adversely by the negative externality

$$MSC =$$

▶ Marginal social cost curve lies ____ the private marginal cost curve (supply curve)

Notes for Marginal Social Cost

Negative Externality

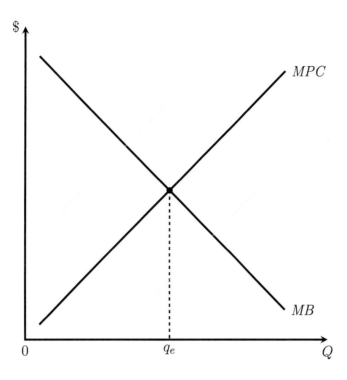

Notes for Negative Externality

If a Negative Externality Exists:

- At every q:
- At every q:
$$MSC - MPC =$$

- The market outcome (q_e):
- The optimal outcome (q^*):
- The quantity produced and consumed is

Negative Externalities and Efficiency Impacts

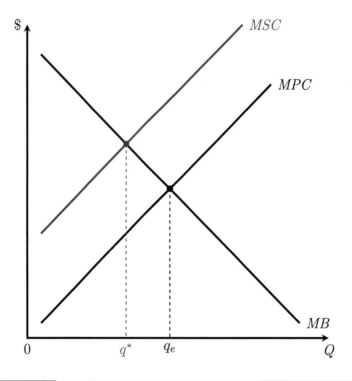

Notes for Negative Externalities and Efficiency Impacts

If a Negative Externality Exists:

- $q_e > q^*$
- Quantities are produced and consumed where
    - This is _____
    - All of the quantities where $q^* < q_i \leq q_e$:

$$MB_{q_i} - MSC_{q_i}$$

- Calculating DWL:

$$DWL =$$

Positive Externalities

▶ Additional benefit to society of consuming a good
  ◇ ⟹ _____ of consumption is larger than the benefit to the consumers of the good
  ◇ Examples

▶ Marginal Private Benefit (MPB)
  ◇ The additional benefit of consuming one more unit for
  ◇ Without externalities

▶ Marginal External Benefit (MEB)
  ◇ The additional cost of consuming one more unit for
  ◇ With externalities

Marginal Social Benefit

▶ Marginal Social Benefit (MSB)
  ◇ Private benefits to the consumers ____ the external benefits to those bystanders affected positively by the positive externality

$$MSB =$$

▶ Marginal social benefit curve lies _____ of the private marginal benefit curve (demand curve)

Positive Externality

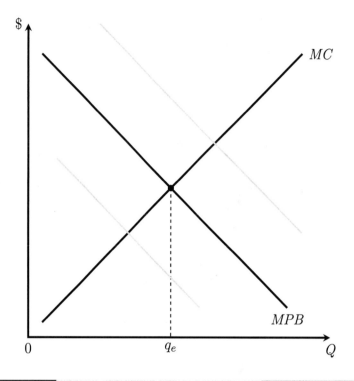

Notes for Positive Externality

If a Positive Externality Exists:

- At every q:
- At every q:
$$MSB - MPB =$$

- The market outcome (q_e):
- The optimal outcome (q^*):
- The quantity produced and consumed by the market is

Positive Externalities and Efficiency Impacts

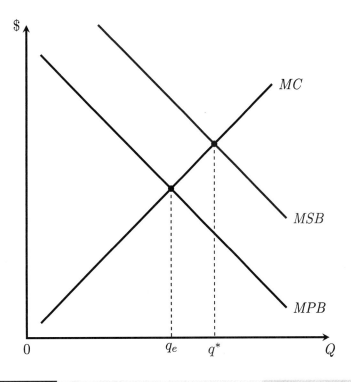

Notes for Positive Externalities and Efficiency Impacts

If a Positive Externality Exists:

- $q_e < q^*$
- Quantities are **not** produced and consumed where
    - This is _____
    - All of the quantities where $q^* > q_i \geq q_e$:

$$MSB_{q_i} - MC_{q_i}$$

- Calculating DWL:

$$DWL =$$

Solutions to the Externality Problem

- The problem: unaddressed externalities lead to deadweight loss
  - ⟹ there are better outcomes

- Two major pathways
  - Command-and-control
    - Regulation and mandates
    - Information problems
  - Market-based policies
    - Changes incentives
    - Taxes, subsidies, tradable permits
    - Much more flexible

Basis for Market-Based Solutions

- Problem with externalities are the spillover effects
  - Consumers/producers do not take account of these effects

- Potential solution: get producers/consumers to consider these spillovers

Definition: Internalizing the Externality

Adjusting incentives so that decision makers take into account all the costs and benefits of their actions, both private and social.

Corrective Taxes

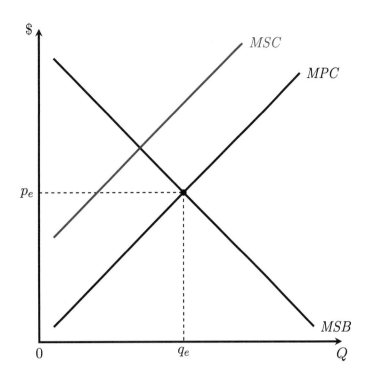

Notes for Corrective Taxes

- **Problem**: At q_e: $MSC_{q_e} > MB_{q_e}$
- **Idea**: Make producers pay the spillover cost of each unit produced
- **Implementation**: Impose a tax on the product that generates the externality
    ◇ How big?

$$\text{tax} =$$

    ◇ $PMC \longrightarrow$
- Pigouvian Tax:
    ◇ Raises revenue for the government
    ◇ Economic efficiency

Corrective Subsidies

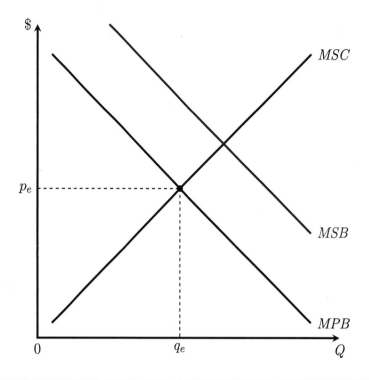

Notes for Corrective Subsidies

- ▶ **Problem**: At q_e: $MSB_{q_e} > MC_{q_e}$
- ▶ **Idea**: Provide consumers with extra value for each unit consumed
- ▶ **Implementation**: Provide a subsidy on the product that generates the externality:
    - ◇ How big?
    $$\text{subsidy} =$$
    - ◇ $MPB \longrightarrow$
- ▶ Pigouvian Subsidy:
    - ◇ Government expenditures (expenditure = subsidy $\times q^*$)
    - ◇ Economic efficiency

Private Solutions to Externalities

> **Definition: Coase Theorem**
>
> If transactions costs are low, _____ will result in an efficient solution to the problem of externalities

- No government intervention is necessary
- Initial distribution of property rights does not matter

Assumptions

- Transactions costs are low
- Property rights are well defined
- Full information about the costs and benefits associated with the externality
- All parties are willing to accept a reasonable agreement

- "Initial distribution of property rights does not matter"
  - Example: who owns the right to clean air
  - No impact on efficiency
- "Transactions costs are low"
  - These are costs in time and other resources that parties incur in the process of agreeing to, and carrying out, an exchange of goods/services

Coase Example

Suppose your neighbor plays music every night and is allowed to do so. Your neighbor plays the music so loud that you have trouble sleeping. Suppose further that your neighbor values playing the music at the aforementioned volume at $300. So long as you value him not playing the music at more than $300 (suppose you value it at $400), you should be able to come to a private solution. That is, you pay him not to play the music.

▶ For example, you can pay him ____ and you would both be ____ better off

▶ Transactions costs should be low here

Externalities Wrap-Up

▶ Externalities exist when there are spillover effects on bystanders

▶ Markets with externalities may not yield the "right outcome"
  ◇ Negative externalities: market produces too much
  ◇ Positive externalities: market produces too little
  ◇ Deadweight loss

▶ Solutions to the externality problem
  ◇ Public policy: taxes and subsidies
  ◇ Private solutions: the Coase Theorem

Chapter 11
Costs and Profit Maximization

Chapter 11: Costs and Profit Maximization Under Competition
Principles of Microeconomics

Prof. Greg Madonia

California State University, Chico

Outline

1. Introduction

2. A Firm's Costs

3. Profit Maximization
   - How a Firm Maximizes Profits

4. Industry Supply Curves

Introduction

- **Assumption**: The goal of firms is to

- To achieve this goal, the firm will need to address 3 questions
    1. When to enter or exit the industry?
    2. How much to produce?
    3. At what price should they sell their output?

- The answer to these questions will be partially determined by what **type** of market the firm must exist in

Competitive Markets

- **Assumption** (for this chapter): firms will be operating in a competitive market

- Competitive Market Characteristics
    1. There are many buyers and sellers
        1.1 Each individual makes up a tiny fraction of the overall market
    2. There are many potential sellers not currently in the market
        2.1 Free entry and exit
    3. Products are effectively identical

Price Taking

- Competitive market characteristics $\implies$ buyers and sellers are **price takers**
    - The market determines the price
    - Buyers can buy as much as they want at the market price
    - Sellers can sell all they want at the market price
        - If sellers charge a higher price, they sell zero
        - Sellers will not charge a lower price
        - $\implies$ The firm's demand curve has a particular shape

The Firm's Demand Curve in a Competitive Market

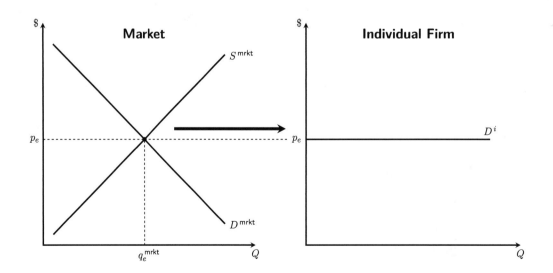

- Price taker $\implies$ individual firm demand (D^i) is **not** a function of how much they produce
- Firm demand is **perfectly elastic** at the market price

How Do Firms Maximize Profit?

▶ The firm's profits
$$\text{Profits} \equiv \pi = TR - TC$$

▶ Total Revenue (TR)
  ◇ Amount of money the firm receives from the sale of its output (q)
$$TR = p \times q$$

▶ Total Cost (TC)
  ◇ Market value of all inputs a firm uses in production
  ◇ Costs as an opportunity cost
    • The cost of something is what you give up to get it

The Firm's Costs of Production

▶ All the opportunity costs incurred when producing its output

Definition: Explicit Costs

Costs that require an outlay of money

  ◇ Examples: Raw materials costs, rent payments, wage bill

Definition: Implicit Costs

Costs that do not require an outlay of money

  ◇ Example: Salary you could have earned in another occupation
  ◇ Ignored by accountants

The Firm's Costs of Production

▶ Total cost
$$TC = \text{explicit costs} + \text{implicit costs}$$

The Costs of Capital as an Opportunity Cost

▶ This is an implicit cost
- Interest income not earned on financial capital
- Not counted as a cost by an accountant

Notes for The Firm's Costs of Production

Accounting vs. Economic Profit

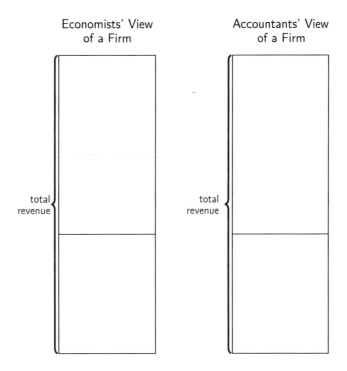

Notes for Accounting vs. Economic Profit

Accounting Profits
- Total revenue minus

Economic Profits
- Total revenue minus
    - Total cost includes both
- π_{econ} $\pi_{accounting}$

Production Function

▶ Relationship between
  1. Quantity of inputs used to make a good, and
  2. Maximum quantity of output of that good, given the level of inputs
▶ Two types of inputs:
  1. Fixed inputs: change in the short run
  2. Variable inputs: be changed in the short run
     - Δs in variable inputs

# of Workers	# of Machines	Output	MP of Labor	Cost of Workers	Cost of Machines	Total Cost
0	2	0	-	0	500	500
1	2	15	15	250	500	750
2	2	40	25	500	500	1000
3	2	80	40	1000	500	1500
4	2	130	50	1750	500	2250
5	2	170	40	2750	500	3250
6	2	200	30	4000	500	4500
7	2	210	10	5500	500	6000
8	2	215	5	7000	500	7500

Notes for Production Function

Production Function

# of Workers	# of Machines	Output	MP of Labor	Cost of Workers	Cost of Machines	Total Cost
0	2	0	-	0	500	500
1	2	15	15	250	500	750
2	2	40	25	500	500	1000
3	2	80	40	1000	500	1500
4	2	130	50	1750	500	2250
5	2	170	40	2750	500	3250
6	2	200	30	4000	500	4500
7	2	210	10	5500	500	6000
8	2	215	5	7000	500	7500

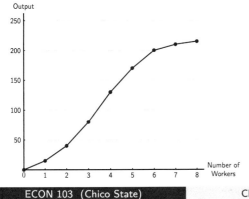

▶ Gets flatter as output increases
  ◇ S-shape
▶ Slope of the production is the **marginal product** of the variable input...

Notes for Production Function

Marginal Product

Definition: Marginal Product

Change in output that arises from an additional unit of input

$$MP_x = \frac{\Delta q}{\Delta x}$$

where x is the quantity of some input (labor, capital, the nth worker, etc...)

▶ MP is the slope of the production function

Notes for Marginal Product

Marginal Product

# of Workers	# of Machines	Output	MP of Labor	Cost of Workers	Cost of Machines	Total Cost
0	2	0	-	0	500	500
1	2	15	15	250	500	750
2	2	40	25	500	500	1000
3	2	80	40	1000	500	1500
4	2	130	50	1750	500	2250
5	2	170	40	2750	500	3250
6	2	200	30	4000	500	4500
7	2	210	10	5500	500	6000
8	2	215	5	7000	500	7500

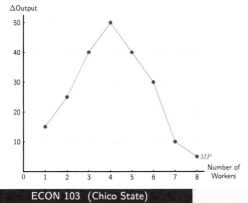

$$MP_x = \frac{\Delta q}{\Delta x}$$

▶ Note: After the 4th worker, MP starts to decline...

Notes for Marginal Product

Law of Diminishing Returns

> **Definition: Law of Diminishing Returns**
>
> The principle that, at some point, adding more of an input to a production process that includes a fixed input will cause the *MP* of the variable input to decline

▶ "...[production function] [g]ets flatter as total output increases"

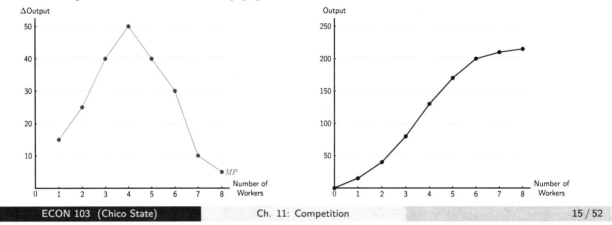

Notes for Law of Diminishing Returns

Total Cost Curve

# of Workers	# of Machines	Output	MP of Labor	Cost of Workers	Cost of Machines	Total Cost
0	2	0	-	0	500	500
1	2	15	15	250	500	750
2	2	40	25	500	500	1000
3	2	80	40	1000	500	1500
4	2	130	50	1750	500	2250
5	2	170	40	2750	500	3250
6	2	200	30	4000	500	4500
7	2	210	10	5500	500	6000
8	2	215	5	7000	500	7500

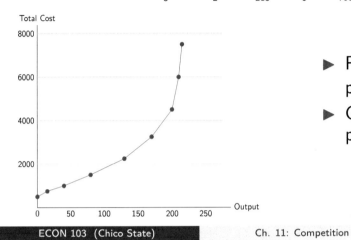

- Relationship between quantity produced and total costs
- Gets steeper as the amount produced arises
  - Caused by the Law of Diminishing Returns

Notes for Total Cost Curve

Time Periods

Definition: Long Run

The time after all exit and entry has occurred

OR

When all inputs in the production process are variable

Definition: Short Run

The time period before exit or entry can occur

OR

When there is at least one fixed input in the production

Costs Defined

Fixed Costs (*FC*)

- Costs associated with
- Costs that do not vary with the quantity of output produced
    - These costs are constant/fixed
- Short-run only

Variable Costs (*VC*)

- Costs associated with
- Costs that vary with the quantity of output produced

Total Cost (TC)

# of Workers	# of Machines	Output	Cost of Workers	Cost of Machines	Total Cost	AFC	AVC	ATC	MC
0	2	0	0	500	500	-	-	-	-
1	2	15	250	500	750	33.33	16.67	50.00	16.67
2	2	40	500	500	1000	12.50	12.50	25.00	10.00
3	2	80	1000	500	1500	6.25	12.50	18.75	12.50
4	2	130	1750	500	2250	3.85	13.46	17.31	15.00
5	2	170	2750	500	3250	2.94	16.18	19.12	25.00
6	2	200	4000	500	4500	2.50	20.00	22.50	41.67
7	2	210	5500	500	6000	2.38	26.19	28.57	150.00
8	2	215	7000	500	7500	2.33	32.56	34.88	300.00

▶ Assume: costs are economic costs
▶ $TC =$
▶ Increases in output $\implies$ costs

Notes for Total Cost (TC)

Average Fixed Costs (AFC)

# of Workers	# of Machines	Output	Cost of Workers	Cost of Machines	Total Cost	AFC	AVC	ATC	MC
0	2	0	0	500	500	-	-	-	-
1	2	15	250	500	750	33.33	16.67	50.00	16.67
2	2	40	500	500	1000	12.50	12.50	25.00	10.00
3	2	80	1000	500	1500	6.25	12.50	18.75	12.50
4	2	130	1750	500	2250	3.85	13.46	17.31	15.00
5	2	170	2750	500	3250	2.94	16.18	19.12	25.00
6	2	200	4000	500	4500	2.50	20.00	22.50	41.67
7	2	210	5500	500	6000	2.38	26.19	28.57	150.00
8	2	215	7000	500	7500	2.33	32.56	34.88	300.00

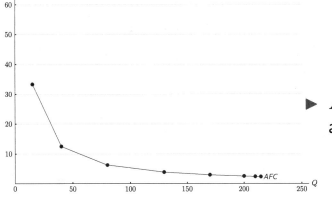

$$AFC = \frac{FC}{q}$$

▶ AFC is _____ as q increases

Notes for Average Fixed Costs (AFC)

Average Variable Costs (AVC)

# of Workers	# of Machines	Output	Cost of Workers	Cost of Machines	Total Cost	AFC	AVC	ATC	MC
0	2	0	0	500	500	-	-	-	-
1	2	15	250	500	750	33.33	16.67	50.00	16.67
2	2	40	500	500	1000	12.50	12.50	25.00	10.00
3	2	80	1000	500	1500	6.25	12.50	18.75	12.50
4	2	130	1750	500	2250	3.85	13.46	17.31	15.00
5	2	170	2750	500	3250	2.94	16.18	19.12	25.00
6	2	200	4000	500	4500	2.50	20.00	22.50	41.67
7	2	210	5500	500	6000	2.38	26.19	28.57	150.00
8	2	215	7000	500	7500	2.33	32.56	34.88	300.00

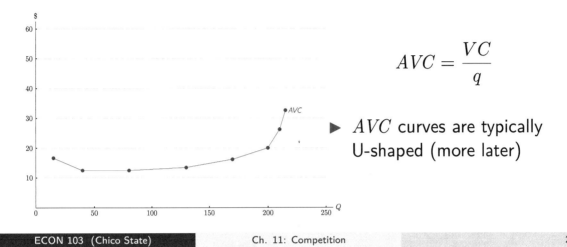

$$AVC = \frac{VC}{q}$$

▶ AVC curves are typically U-shaped (more later)

Notes for Average Variable Costs (AVC)

Average Total Cost (ATC)

# of Workers	# of Machines	Output	Cost of Workers	Cost of Machines	Total Cost	AFC	AVC	ATC	MC
0	2	0	0	500	500	-	-	-	-
1	2	15	250	500	750	33.33	16.67	50.00	16.67
2	2	40	500	500	1000	12.50	12.50	25.00	10.00
3	2	80	1000	500	1500	6.25	12.50	18.75	12.50
4	2	130	1750	500	2250	3.85	13.46	17.31	15.00
5	2	170	2750	500	3250	2.94	16.18	19.12	25.00
6	2	200	4000	500	4500	2.50	20.00	22.50	41.67
7	2	210	5500	500	6000	2.38	26.19	28.57	150.00
8	2	215	7000	500	7500	2.33	32.56	34.88	300.00

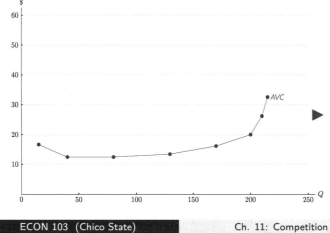

$$ATC = \frac{TC}{q}$$

▶ Like the AVC curve, ATC curves are also typically U-shaped (more later)

Notes for Average Total Cost (ATC)

Relationship between the Average Cost Curves

Recall:
$$TC = FC + VC$$

So,
$$\frac{TC}{q} = \frac{FC + VC}{q}$$
$$\frac{TC}{q} = \frac{FC}{q} + \frac{VC}{q}$$

$$ATC = AFC + AVC$$

Notes for Relationship between the Average Cost Curves

Relationship Between Average Cost Curves

$$ATC = AFC + AVC$$

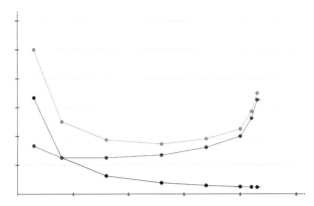

▶ Things to Note:
- Visually, the ATC curve will lie _____ the AVC curve
- $ATC - AVC = AFC$
  - AFC constant declining $\implies$ distance between ATC and AVC gets _____ as q _____

Notes for Relationship Between Average Cost Curves

Marginal Cost (MC)

# of Workers	# of Machines	Output	Cost of Workers	Cost of Machines	Total Cost	AFC	AVC	ATC	MC
0	2	0	0	500	500	-	-	-	-
1	2	15	250	500	750	33.33	16.67	50.00	16.67
2	2	40	500	500	1000	12.50	12.50	25.00	10.00
3	2	80	1000	500	1500	6.25	12.50	18.75	12.50
4	2	130	1750	500	2250	3.85	13.46	17.31	15.00
5	2	170	2750	500	3250	2.94	16.18	19.12	25.00
6	2	200	4000	500	4500	2.50	20.00	22.50	41.67
7	2	210	5500	500	6000	2.38	26.19	28.57	150.00
8	2	215	7000	500	7500	2.33	32.56	34.88	300.00

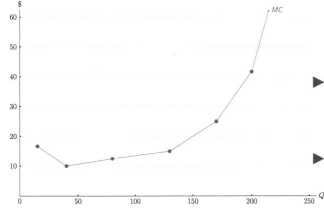

$$MC = \frac{\Delta TC}{\Delta q}$$

▶ At some point, the MC curve increases due to the

▶ Often has a "checkmark" or "Nike swoosh" shape

Notes for Marginal Cost (MC)

Relationship between MC and ATC

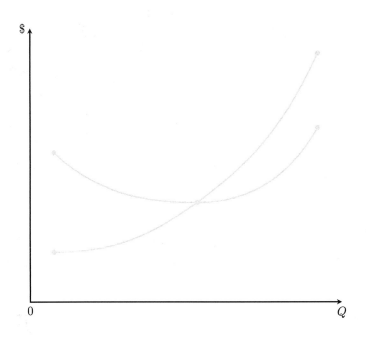

Notes for Relationship between MC and ATC

1. If $MC < ATC$
   ◇ ATC is
2. If $MC > ATC$
   ◇ ATC is

▶ (1) and (2) $\implies$:
   ◇ ATC is
   ◇ The MC curve crosses the ATC curve at the _____ of the ATC

▶ MC also crosses the AVC at its minimum
▶ AVC is also u-shaped for the same reasons

Putting It All Together

# of Workers	# of Machines	Output	Cost of Workers	Cost of Machines	Total Cost	AFC	AVC	ATC	MC
0	2	0	0	500	500	-	-	-	-
1	2	15	250	500	750	33.33	16.67	50.00	16.67
2	2	40	500	500	1000	12.50	12.50	25.00	10.00
3	2	80	1000	500	1500	6.25	12.50	18.75	12.50
4	2	130	1750	500	2250	3.85	13.46	17.31	15.00
5	2	170	2750	500	3250	2.94	16.18	19.12	25.00
6	2	200	4000	500	4500	2.50	20.00	22.50	41.67
7	2	210	5500	500	6000	2.38	26.19	28.57	150.00
8	2	215	7000	500	7500	2.33	32.56	34.88	300.00

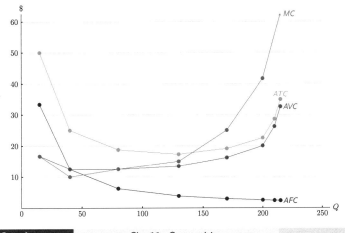

Notes for Putting It All Together

A Firm's Costs

Better Looking Cost Curves and Wrap-Up

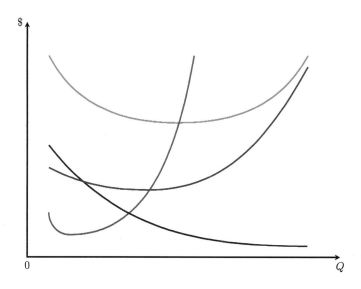

A Firm's Costs

Notes for Better Looking Cost Curves and Wrap-Up

- The ATC curve lies above the AVC curve
  ◇ $ATC = AFC + AVC$
- The MC curve crosses both the ATC and AVC curves at their respective minimums
- AFC is constantly declining as output increases
- As q increases, the distance between the ATC curve and the AVC curve will decrease
  ◇ $ATC - AVC = AFC$

TR, AR, and MR for a Competitive Firm

Q	P	TR	AR	MR
0	14		-	-
1	14			
2	14			
3	14			
4	14			
5	14			
6	14			
7	14			
8	14			

Notes for TR, AR, and MR for a Competitive Firm

- **Total Revenue** (TR)
$$TR =$$
  ◇ p is constant $\implies$ TR is _____ to the amount of output

- **Average Revenue** (AR)
$$AR =$$

- **Marginal Revenue** (MR)
$$MR =$$

- For firms in a competitive market:

Measuring a Firm's Profits

▶ **Firm's Goal**: maximize profits

$$\pi = TR - TC$$
$$= p \times q - TC$$

dividing both sides by q

$$\frac{\pi}{q} = \frac{p \times q - TC}{q} = \frac{p \times q}{q} - \frac{TC}{q}$$
$$\frac{\pi}{q} = p - ATC \quad \text{(profits per unit)}$$

since $TC/q = ATC$. Finally, multiplying both sides by q,

$$\pi = (p - ATC) \times q$$

▶ If $p > ATC \implies$ \qquad and if $p < ATC \implies$

Visualizing Profits

A Firm with Profits ($\pi > 0$) \qquad **A Firm with Losses ($\pi < 0$)**

▶ Height of the rectangle:
▶ Base of the rectangle:

Maximizing Profits

▶ Firm is a price taker $\implies$
   ◇ $\implies$ They max profit by

▶ Rules:
  1. Produce the quantity where total revenue minus total cost is greatest, and/or
  2. Compare marginal revenue with marginal cost
     - $MR > MC \implies$
     - $MR < MC \implies$
     - Profit is maximized at the q where

Profit Maximization: Discrete Quantities Example

Q	P	TR	TC	π	AR	MR	$-$	MC	$=$	$\Delta\pi$
0	14	0	4	-4	-	-		-		-
1	14	14	12	2	14	14	—	8	=	+6
2	14	28	18	10	14	14	—	6	=	+8
3	14	42	28	14	14	14	—	10	=	+4
4	14	56	40	16	14	14	—	12	=	+2
5	14	70	54	16	14	14	—	14	=	+0
6	14	84	70	14	14	14	—	16	=	-2
7	14	98	90	8	14	14	—	20	=	-6
8	14	112	118	-6	14	14	—	28	=	-14

The Marginal Cost Curve and the Firm's Supply Decision

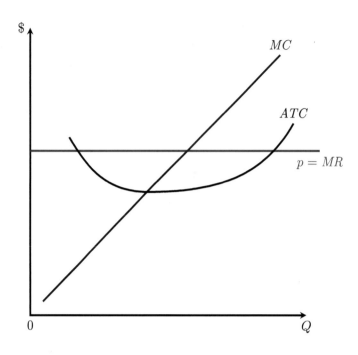

Notes for The Marginal Cost Curve and the Firm's Supply Decision

- MC curve is (eventually) upward sloping

- $p = MR$

- q_1: MC_{q_1} MR
  - $\implies$

- q_2: MC_{q_2} MR
  - $\implies$

- $q_{\pi\max}$ is the q where
  - profit is _____
  - This is an _____

- $\pi =$ ×

Marginal Cost as the Firm's Supply Curve

Since $p = MR$,

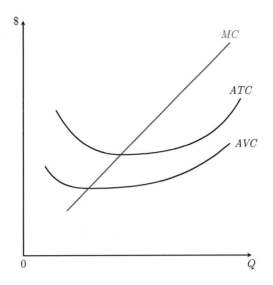

A firm's *MC* curve is its supply curve (mostly)

When is a Firm's MC Curve **NOT** Its Supply Curve?

Two situations where the firm's marginal cost curve is not its supply curve

1. Shutdown
   - **Short-run** decision not to produce anything
   - Firm still pays fixed costs even if they shutdown

2. Exit
   - **Long-run** decision to leave the market
   - Firm does not have to pay any costs after they exit the market

Shutdown Rules

- A firm will shutdown if:
  - ◇ $TR < VC$, which is the same as
  - ◇ $p < AVC$
- Shut-down price $p_{sd} = \min\{AVC\}$

Intuition:

Scenario 1:

q	p	TR	VC	FC	π
0	25	0	0	1000	
1	25	25	50	1000	

- Optimal $q =$
  - ◇ _____

Scenario 2:

q	p	TR	VC	FC	π
0	75	0	0	1000	
1	75	75	50	1000	

- Optimal $q =$
  - ◇ _____

Notes for Shutdown Rules

The Competitive Firm's Short-run Supply Curve

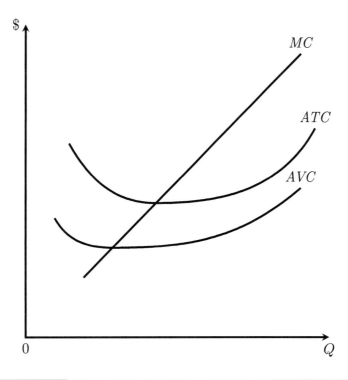

Notes for The Competitive Firm's Short-run Supply Curve

- ▶ Shutdown price
  - ◇ $p_{\text{sd}} =$

- ▶ Break-even price
  - ◇ $p_{\text{be}} =$

- ▶ Firm's S-R Supply Curve
  - ◇ The MC curve above the _____ curve, and _____ otherwise

- ▶ Operating at a loss
  - ◇ $p_{\text{sd}} \leq p <$
  - ◇ Why would a firm operate if they are earning negative profits...?

Sunk Costs

> **Definition: Sunk Cost**
>
> A cost that

- Examples: salaries, contracts, non-refundable tickets

- In the production context, fixed costs and sunk costs are equivalent

- Ignore them when making decisions
  ◇ Relationship between p and AVC, **not** p and ATC
  ◇ Choose the q where

- Sunk cost only exist in the short-run...

Industry-Level Supply Curves

- So far: firm-level decisions

- Now: how do firm-level entry-and-exit decisions shape the industry-level supply curve?

- Three categories of industries by cost structure. As industry output increases, costs can:
  1. Increase
  2. Remain constant
  3. Decrease

Increasing Cost Industries

> **Definition: Increasing Cost Industry**
>
> As output increases, costs in the industry increase, and vice-versa.

▶ Industry-level supply curve is _____

▶ Causes
- As output increases, _____ methods of production must be employed
- There are significant _____ in the production process
- Spillover effects
  - Industries that use large amounts of output from an increasing cost industry will also be an increasing cost industry

Notes for Increasing Cost Industries

Increasing Cost Industries

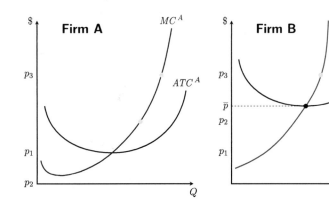
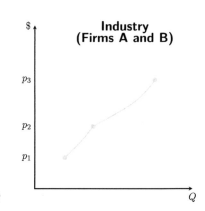

Notes for Increasing Cost Industries

- $p < p_1$: market quantity

- $p = p_1$: market quantity

- $p = p_2$: market quantity

- $p > \bar{p}$:

- $\bar{p} < p = p_3$: market quantity

Constant Cost Industries

> **Definition: Constant Cost Industries**
>
> As output changes, costs in the industry _____

▶ Most appropriate for competitive markets
  ◇ Meets all the assumptions (see earlier in the slides)

▶ Requires that the demand for the most important inputs is relatively small
  ◇ Price of inputs _____ very much as output changes in the industry

Industry Supply In a Constant Cost Industry

In the long-run...

▶ Firms are able to enter and exit the market

▶ If $p > ATC \implies \pi > 0 \implies$

▶ If $p < ATC \implies \pi < 0 \implies$

▶ Process of entry and exit ceases when:
  ◇ Firms still in the market make
  ◇ This is the q where

Why Do Competitive Firms Stay in Business if They Make Zero Economic Profit?

- $\pi = TR - TC$

- For economists, total cost includes **all costs** – including

  - Economic profit $> 0 \implies$

  - Assumptions $\implies$ anyone can mimic the production process of someone who is making economic profit

- Zero-profit equilibrium
  - Economic profit is zero
  - Accounting profit is

A Competitive Market in Long-run Equilibrium

- Every long-run equilibrium is a short-run equilibrium

- Zero economic profit
  - No incentive to enter or exit

- $p = \min\{ATC\}$

- How do we get changes in equilibrium?
  - Changes in demand or supply
    - Exception: $\pi = 0 \implies$

Equilibrium to Equilibrium

	Action	**Note**
	Long-run equilibrium $\implies \pi = 0$	start
	Δ demand P.I.N.T.E.	
$\implies$		
$\implies$		
$\implies$		
$\implies$		remember: $\pi = (p - ATC) \times q$
$\implies$		
$\implies$		supply P.I.N.T.E.
$\implies$		
$\implies$		
$\implies$		
$\implies$		
$\implies$		end

Notes for Equilibrium to Equilibrium

213

Industry Supply Curves

A Decrease in Demand in the S-R and the L-R

Initial condition...

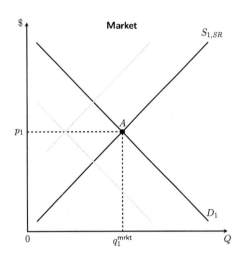
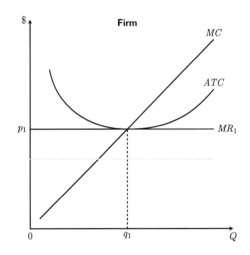

At equilibrium firms are neither exiting nor entering the market as $\pi = 0$

Industry Supply Curves

A Decrease in Demand in the S-R and the L-R

Demand ↓ and there is a short-run change in the market equilibrium

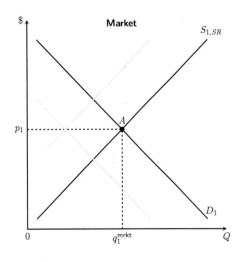
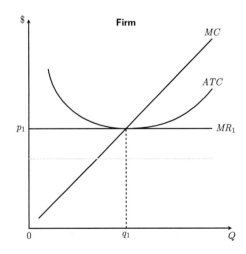

Short-run losses will provide incentive for some firms to exit the market...

A Decrease in Demand in the S-R and the L-R

Firms exiting will cause the short-run supply curve to decrease

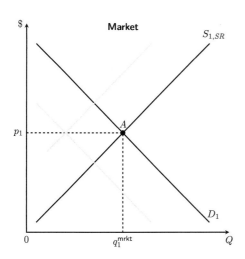
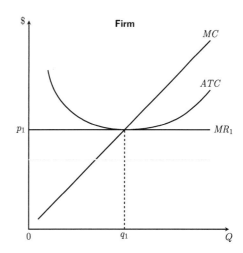

Firms exiting ⟶ prices ↑ until $\pi = 0$ **which occurs at the original price**.

A Decrease in Demand in the S-R and the L-R

Firms exiting will cause the short-run supply curve to decrease

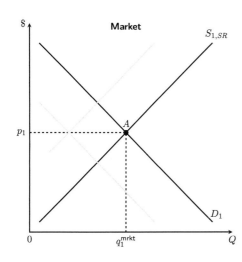
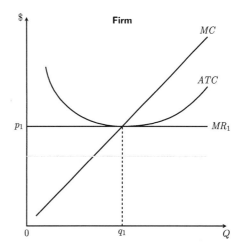

Points A and C are points on the long-run supply curve

Industry Supply Curve in Constant Cost Industry

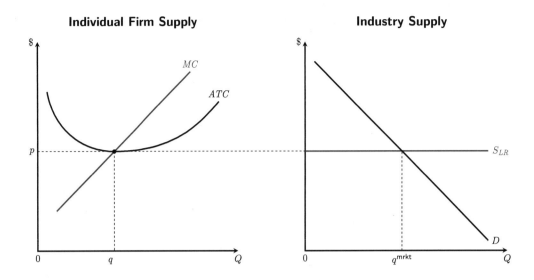

- At equilibrium:
- Long-run changes in price ____ come through changes in costs

Decreasing Cost Industry

Definition: Decreasing Cost Industry

As output increases, costs in the industry _____ and vice-versa

- Industry-level supply curve is _____

- Causes
  - Increasing specialization of inputs
  - "Clustering" of firms
    - Akron, Ohio: Rubber capital of the world
    - Silicon Valley

- Often temporary
  - Returns to constant, or increasing, cost industry

Decreasing Cost Industry

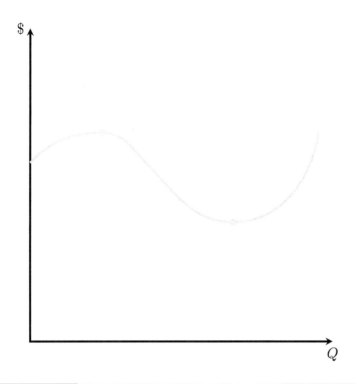

Notes for Decreasing Cost Industry

- $0 < q < q_1$:

- $q_1 < q < q_2$:

- $q > q_2$:

Chapter Wrap-Up

- ▶ The firm's goal is to maximize profits

- ▶ In a competitive industry, the firm does not choose price but they can control costs

- ▶ Firms maximize profits by choosing the quantity where marginal revenue is equal to marginal cost

- ▶ Different industries have different industry-level cost structures

Chapter 13

Monopoly

Chapter 13: Monopoly
Principles of Microeconomics

Prof. Greg Madonia

California State University, Chico

Outline

1. Introduction

2. Production and Pricing Decisions

3. Monopolies and Efficiency

4. Why Do Monopolies Arise?

5. Government Response to Monopoly Behavior

Introduction

- Competitive firms are on one end of the market-structure spectrum

- On the other end of that spectrum: monopolies

- Competitive markets are usually the best market for consumers and economic efficiency

- This chapter: how monopolies behave, the reasons that monopolies arise, and the impact on consumers and economic efficiency

What is a Monopoly?

Definition: Monopoly (Definition 1)

A **monopoly** is a firm that is a sole seller of a product _____
_____

- Examples:
    - Professional baseball in the US (MLB)
    - Electricity (PG&E)

- Monopolies are
    - Choose the price for their good

What is a Monopoly?

> **Definition: Market Power**
>
> The power to raise price _____ without fear that other firms will

> **Definition: Monopoly (Definition 2)**
>
> A firm with

▶ More examples:
  ◇ Aluminum (Alcoa)
  ◇ iPhone (Apple)

Initial Assumption

> **Definition: Single-price Monopoly**
>
> A **single-price monopoly** is a monopolist that charges the same price to all consumers for all units

▶ Monopolist cannot differentiate between consumers based on how much they would pay
  ◇ In the "real world" this has become rare

▶ Examples:
  ◇ PG&E and other utilities
  ◇ Driver's license
  ◇ Toll Road
  ◇ iPhone (?)

Competitive Firm Revenue Curves: Reminder

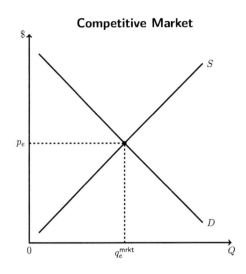

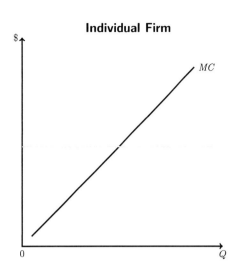

- Firms in a Perfectly Competitive Market
  ◇ One of many firms where goods are identical $\implies$ they face a

$$p =$$

Monopolies Face the Entire Market Demand

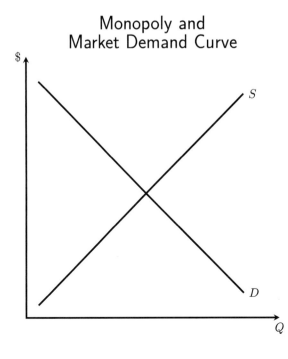

- Firms in the competitive market serve a very small portion of the overall market

- Monopolies face the entire market
  ◇ $\implies$ the market demand curve

  ◇ Can no longer assume

Monopoly Revenue Curves

Q	P	TR	AR	MR
0	200		-	-
1	175			
2	150			
3	125			
4	100			
5	75			
6	50			
7	25			
8	0			

Notes for Monopoly Revenue Curves

- $TR =$
- $AR =$
- Marginal Revenue (MR)
    - Change in total revenue from an additional unit of output

    $$MR =$$

    - MR _____ p
        - Demand is downward sloping $\implies$ monopolist must lower price _____ to sell an additional unit
    - MR can be _____

The Monopolist's MR Curve

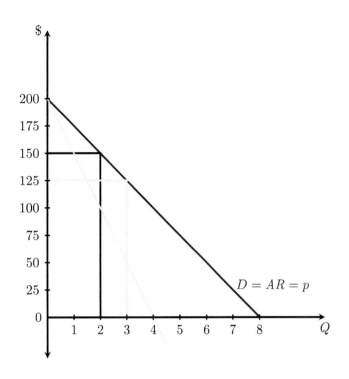

Notes for The Monopolist's MR Curve

When a monopolist lowers price to sell more quantity

- Price Effect
  - p is lower
  - _____ in TR

- Output Effect
  - q is higher
  - _____ in TR

- Marginal revenue
  - Combination of both effects

- Downward sloping demand $\implies$ price effect > 0 $\implies$ _____ for all q
  - In perfect competition: price effect $= 0$

Profit Maximization

▶ If $MR > MC \implies$ _____ production

▶ If $MR < MC \implies$ _____ production

▶ To maximize profits...
  1. Produce the quantity where
     - In a discrete q setting, may have to produce at the last q where

  2. Choose _____ p that will sell all the q where $MR = MC$
     - Monopolies are price makers

Notes for Profit Maximization

Profit Maximization for a Monopolist (Visually)

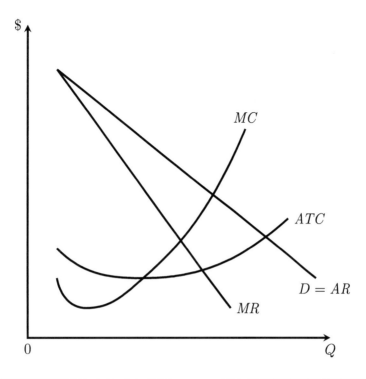

Notes for Profit Maximization for a Monopolist (Visually)

- Produce q where $MR = MC$

- Choose the p on the _____ for q_{mon}

- Monopoly:
  - _____ =
  - In perfect competition: $p = MC$

- Monopoly profits:

Mark-up Size and Elasticity

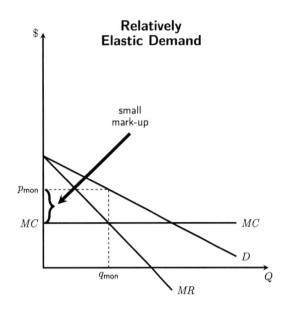
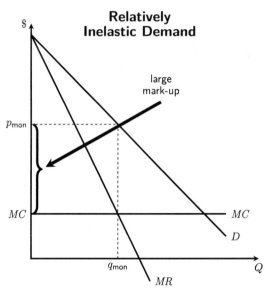

▶ As demand becomes more _____, mark-up becomes _____

▶ Example: Necessities versus luxuries

Monopolies and Efficiency

▶ Monopolies charge higher prices (mark-up) and produce fewer units than competitive industries

▶ Potential efficiency concerns:
  ◇ Higher prices
    • Not necessarily an efficiency concern: transfer from consumer to producers
  ◇ Lower quantity
    • Big concern: is the monopolist not producing quantities that "should" be produced?

Welfare Economics Reminder

- ▶ Total Surplus
  - ◇ Economic well-being of buyers and sellers in a market
  - ◇ $TS = CS + PS$

- ▶ Consumer Surplus
  - ◇ $CS_i = MB_i - p$, for all units consumed

- ▶ Producer Surplus
  - ◇ $PS_i = p - MC_i$, for all units produced

- ▶ Maximizing Total Surplus
  - ◇ Produce q where MC curve intersects demand ($MC = MB$): q^*
  - ◇ $p = MC$ yields this result

Notes for Welfare Economics Reminder

Welfare Results from a Monopoly Market

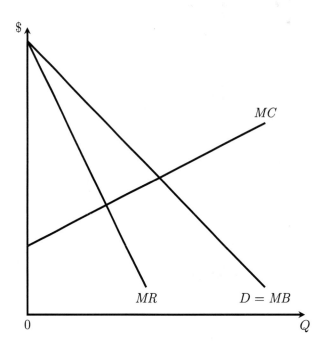

Notes for Welfare Results from a Monopoly Market

- Produce q where $MR = MC$
  ◇ q_{mon} q^*
- Charge p $MC = MR$
  ◇ _____

- _____
  ◇ There are quantities not produced and consumed where
  ◇ Calculation:

Additional Costs of a Monopoly Market

- Upstream monopolies can be especially destructive

- Monopolies can be the result of government corruption

- Examples
  - Post-USSR Russia: Utility companies were sold for pennies on the dollar
  - US: MLB

Benefit of a Monopoly

- Monopoly power can lead to a firm investing in Research and Development (R&D)

- Patents and Copyrights
  - Patent: Sole right to produce a good or service
  - Copyright: Sole right to use a piece of intellectual property

- Without the incentive of monopoly profit's, firms will invest less
  - $\implies$ less new stuff for consumers

- Alternatives to increase market efficiency
  - Prizes for new innovations
  - Patent buy outs
    - Requires tax spending...
    - What's the price...?

Why Do Monopolies Exist?

▶ Four major reasons why monopolies exist
1. Barriers to Entry
2. Network Effects
3. Innovation
4. The Production Process

Barriers to Entry

▶ Monopolies can earn long-run economic profits even when costs are constant or declining

▶ Firms may want to enter the market and compete with the monopolist,

Definition: Barriers to Entry

Factors that _____ to new firms of entering an industry.

Barriers to Entry Factors

1. Government Regulation
   - Patents and Copyrights
   - Laws
     - MLB, USPS

2. Ownership of a key resource
   - The monopolist (almost) completely owns an input that is necessary to produce the output
     - Example: Alcoa and aluminum, DeBeers and diamonds

3. Switching costs
   - The non-monetary cost of switching to a competitor is "too high" for most consumers
     - Microsoft office, Apple vs. Windows

Network Effects

Definition: Network Effects

A product with network effects has its value to an individual consumer increase as the _____ and vice-versa

▶ Examples:
  - Social media, credit cards, fandoms...

▶ Firms may want to enter but may not "steal" enough _____ from the pre-existing firms to be profitable

Why Do Monopolies Arise?

Innovation

▶ As a monopolist innovates, potential competitors will find it harder to duplicate

▶ Trade-off for consumers
  ◇ Pro:

  ◇ Con:

Why Do Monopolies Arise?

The Production Process

▶ Sometimes a single firm can produce output at a lower average cost than can multiple firms
  ◇ **Natural Monopoly**
  ◇ Example: Utilities
  ◇ Arise because of economies of scale

Definition: Economies of Scale

The advantages of large-scale production that reduce average cost as quantity increases.

Natural Monopolies and Economies of Scale

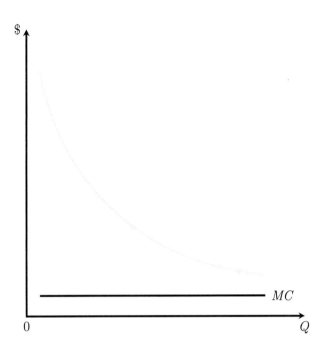

Notes for Natural Monopolies and Economies of Scale

- Natural Monopoly Characteristics:
  - ____ fixed costs and ____ marginal costs
    - $\implies$ _____

- Let X be the amount desired by the market
  - Also, let $q_1 = q_2 = \frac{X}{2}$
  - $ATC_X \qquad ATC_{q_1}, ATC_{q_2}$

- A single firm can supply a good/sevice to an entire market at a ____ (average) cost than can multiple firms

Governments and Monopolies

- Most instances: monopolies are bad for consumers
  - ⟹ rational basis for government intervention

- Government tools for intervention
  1. Price controls
  2. Direct government ownership
  3. Legal mechanisms
     - Antitrust law

Notes for Governments and Monopolies

Monopolies and Price Controls

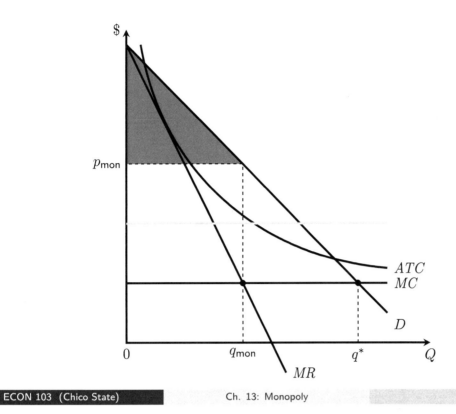

Notes for Monopolies and Price Controls

▶ Monopoly outcome
- ◇ p_{mon} MC: mark-up
- ◇ q_{mon} q^*

▶ Government imposes a binding price ceiling
- ◇ p
- ◇ q
- ◇ CS

▶ Note: q_c q^*

Price Control Limits For a Natural Monopoly

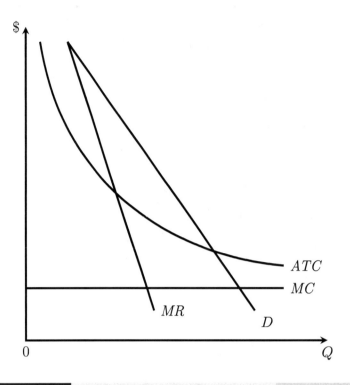

Notes for Price Control Limits For a Natural Monopoly

- ▶ Marginal cost pricing
    - ◇ Government requires the monopolist to charge $p =$
    - ◇ Losses if the market is too small
        - If q^* is where

- ▶ Average cost pricing
    - ◇ Allow the firm to charge the average cost (plus a little more) of q^*
    - ◇ Problem: does not give the firm incentive to lower costs

Government Ownership

▶ Another tool for the government is to directly own a monopoly market

▶ Utilities

▶ Pro: Utilities are often "necessities" and a monopolist exploiting market power is unpopular

▶ Cons
  ◇ No incentive for innovation
  ◇ No incentive to be efficient

Antitrust Laws

▶ Idea: increase competition through law

▶ Important laws
  ◇ Sherman Antitrust Act (1890)
  ◇ Clayton Antitrust Act (1914)

▶ Prevents anti-consumer mergers

▶ Break-up non-competitive companies

▶ Makes co-ordination between firms to set prices illegal

Wrap-Up

▶ Monopolies are the sole producer in some market

▶ Higher prices, smaller quantity, and loss of economic efficiency

▶ Monopolies can earn long-run economic profit
  ◇ Protected by barriers to entry, network effects, innovative practices, and/or the production process (natural monopolies)

▶ Government has various tools to improve economic efficiency

Chapter 15

Oligopoly

Chapter 15: Oligopoly
Principles of Microeconomics

Prof. Greg Madonia

California State University, Chico

Outline

1. Introduction

2. Game Theory
   - The Prisoners' Dilemma
   - More Simultaneous Games
   - Repeated Simultaneous Games
   - Sequential Games
   - Extra Sequential Games

3. More Business Strategies

Imperfect Competition

▶ Lies between perfect competition and monopoly

▶ Two types of markets
  ◇ Oligopoly (this chapter)
  ◇ Monopolistic Competition (different chapter)

Characteristic	Monopolistic Competition	Oligopoly
# of Sellers	Many	Few
Product Differentiation	Yes	Not Really...
Barriers to Entry	No	Typically

▶ Oligopoly examples:
▶ Monopolistic competition examples:

Oligopoly Overview

Definition: Oligopoly

A market that is dominated by a small number of firms.

Definition: Cartel

A group of suppliers who try to act as if they were a monopoly.

▶ Monopoly with multiple production centers
  ◇ Recall: Monopoly $\implies q_{mon} < q_{comp} \implies p_{mon} > p_{comp}$

Introduction

Oligopoly Overview

- ▶ Oligopolies that do not (cannot) form a cartel **usually** will still have reduced quantity and higher prices than competitive industries
  - ◇ $q_{mon} < q_{olig} < q_{comp} \implies p_{mon} > p_{olig} > p_{comp}$

- ▶ Why wouldn't oligipoly firms always work together?
  - ◇ Illegal in some countries/markets
  - ◇ Firms face a trade-off

- ▶ Trade-off
  - ◇ Cooperate and maximize **joint** payoff
  - ◇ Pursue self-interest
    - $q_i \uparrow \implies q_{olig} \uparrow \implies p \downarrow$
    - Prices drop for **all** oligopolists when one oligopolist increases production

- ▶ Need a new analysis method: **game theory**

Game Theory

A Different Form of Analysis

- ▶ So far, we have used **marginal analysis**
  - ◇ Choose the q where $MR = MC$...
  - ◇ Relatively easy to do when choices are **independent**

- ▶ What happens when choices are **interdependent**?
  - ◇ Choices are strategic: your choice depends on the choices of others

Definition: Strategic Decision Making

Decision making in situations that are interactive

Game Theory

A Different Form of Analysis

- ▶ Examples of strategic situations
  - ◇ A firm knows that if they offer a high price competitors may enter the market, but if they offer a low price competitors may not enter
  - ◇ The US is deciding whether to lower tariffs on a country that has committed human rights abuses. This other country may retaliate with trade sanctions if the US does not lower the tariffs
  - ◇ Two roommates are individually thinking about washing the dishes. Both roommates want the dishes cleaned, but both also hate washing dishes

- ▶ **Game theory** is useful for these scenarios

Game Theory

Game Theory

- ▶ Game theory is an analytical framework that is useful when the choices of economic agents are interdependent

- ▶ Each oligopolist faces a trade-off
  - ◇ Cooperate
  - ◇ Pursue own self interests

- ▶ The oligopolist will make their best decision based on what they **think** the other oligopolists will do

Definition: Nash Equilibrium

> **Definition: Nash Equilibrium**
>
> An equilibrium in which each economic agent (player) chooses the _____ given the strategies of the other economic agents

- We will focus on "pure strategies"
  - Players either always do some action or never do some action
- Equilibrium Criterion
  - No player wants to
- Cooperative Equilibrium
  - Cooperate to increase their mutual (joint) payoffs/outcomes
- Noncooperative (competitve) Equilibrium
  - Do not cooperate, but pursue their own self-interest

The Prisoners' Dilemma

- Game between two captured prisoners
- Meant to show the trade-off between cooperating and self-interest

Setup
- Two players: Prisoner 1 and Prisoner 2
- Each prisoner can choose between one of two actions: Talk and Silent
  - Game is played simultaneously
- After the players have chosen their action, they receive their payoff
  - Number of years of freedom gained
    - For example, -2 is going to jail for 2 years
    - Higher values are better

Setup

▶ Matrix notation for the Prisoners' Dilemma
  ◇ Player 1 is the "row player" and Player 2 is the "column player"

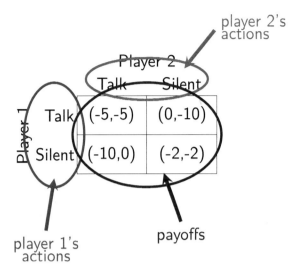

▶ Each cell represent both players' payoffs
  ◇ (Player 1's payoff, Player 2's payoff)

Solving the Prisoners' Dilemma

Let's look for an equilibrium. That is, an outcome where neither player wants to change their action (deviate) **given the choice of the other player**

	Player 2	
	Talk	Silent
Player 1 Talk	(-5,-5)	(0,-10)
Silent	(-10,0)	(-2,-2)

▶ Solution is
  ◇ The payoff for each player is that they _____
  ◇ This is a _____
    • No player will deviate

Outcome of the Prisoners' Dilemma

- The best joint outcome is {Silent, Silent}
  ◇ Total of 4 years in jail

- However, self-interest $\implies$ {Talk, Talk}, given the setup
  ◇ Total of 10 years in jail (5 each)

> **Definition: Prisoners' Dilemma**
>
> A situation in which the pursuit of individual interest leads to a group outcome that is in the interest of no one; the negative counterpart to the invisible hand.

- Each player has a dominant strategy

Definition: Dominant Strategy

> **Definition: Dominant Strategy**
>
> A strategy that is best for the economic agent _____ of the actions chosen by the other economic agents

- In the Prisoners' Dilemma, each player has a dominant strategy:

- If both players have a dominant strategy, like in the Prisoners' Dilemma, then there is a Nash equilibrium where these strategies overlap

Application: OPEC

▶ OPEC: Oil Producing and Exporting Countries
  ◇ 13 members (2022)
  ◇ Produces 44 percent of the world's crude oil (2018)
  ◇ A cartel

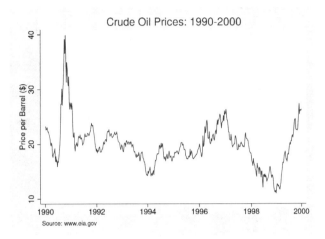

▶ Variation in prices: evidence that members were cheating

Modeling OPEC Member Decisions

Let's look for dominant strategies and Nash equilibria. Payoffs are (Congo, Gabon)

	Gabon High	Gabon Low
Congo High	(4,4)	(7,2)
Congo Low	(2,7)	(10,10)

▶ Dominant strategies?:
▶ Nash equilibria?:
▶ This is the

Another Game

Let's look for dominant strategies and Nash equilibria. Payoffs are (Player A, Player B)

	Player B	
	Left	Right
Player A Up	(-5,4)	(12,8)
Down	(10,11)	(7,10)

- Dominant strategies?:
- Nash equilibria?:

Yet Another Game

Again, let's look for dominant strategies and Nash equilibria. Payoffs are (Batter, Pitcher)

	Pitcher	
	Curve	Fast
Batter Curve	(1,-1)	(-1,1)
Fast	(-1,1)	(1,-1)

- Dominant strategies?:
- Nash equilibria?:

A Retail Game

Market for HDTVs:

	Walmart $1,000	Walmart $800
Best Buy $1,000	($50K, $50K)	($20K, $70K)
Best Buy $800	($70K, $20K)	($44K, $44K)

- Dominant Strategies?:
    ◇
- Nash Equilibria?:
    ◇

Trying To Get To the Cooperative Equilibrium

In the Retail Game
- Nash Equilibrium is $\{\$800, \$800\}$ yielding a payoff of \$44,000
    ◇ If this game is played once, this will definitely be the outcome
    ◇ If this game is played repeatedly, each firm loses out on _____ each time

Repeated Games
- If the game is played repeatedly, there is a potential to get to the cooperative outcome
    ◇ Retaliation strategies
        • Gives incentive to collude

Collusion

▶ In the US, collusion between firms is illegal, but firms still engage in **tacit collusion**

> **Definition: Tacit Collusion**
>
> When firms limit competition with one another but do so without explicit agreement or communication.

▶ Example: Price matching
  ◇ Firms will advertise a price and then offer to "beat" the prices of their competitors if they offer lower prices

Price Matching

	Walmart $1,000	Walmart $800
Best Buy $1,000	($50K,$50K)	($60K,$0)
Best Buy $800	($0,$60K)	($44K,$44K)

▶ Dominant Strategies?: $1,000 for each player
▶ Nash eq: $\{\$1{,}000, \$1{,}000\}$
  ◇ The cooperate equilibrium

Repeating Oil Production Game

Two oil producers: Saudia Arabia (large producer) and Nigeria (small producer), who decide on how much oil to produce in a given month (High or Low – note that Saudia Arabia's Low is greater than Nigeria's High)

		Nigeria	
		Low	High
Saudi Arabia	Low	($100M,$15M)	($75M,$25M)
	High	($80M,$3M)	($60M,$5M)

- Dominant Strategies?:
    ◇ Saudia Arabia:
    ◇ Nigeria:
- Nash Equilibria?:
    ◇

Repeated Oil Production Game Outcomes

- At the Nash Equilibrium Saudia Arabia loses:

- Saudi Arabia could "bribe" Nigeria to play "Low" (for example, pay them $11M per month) – both are better off
    ◇ Does this collusion hold?

- If Nigeria consistently cheats, Saudia Arabia could employ a

    ◇ Saudi Arabia's punishment strategy:
    ◇ This strategy could force the non-Nash Equilibrium of
    ◇ Nigeria is not best-off given Saudi Arabia's choice in that time period

Simultaneous Games Wrap-Up

▶ Strategic decisions
  ◇ A player's choice depends on the actions of other players

▶ A Nash equilibrium occurs where no player wants to change their action give the choice of the other player(s). This can lead to:
  ◇ Cooperative equilibriums
  ◇ Noncooperative equilibriums

▶ Highlights the tension between _____

▶ Nash equilibria can be "escaped" if there are incentives to do so

▶ A dominant strategy is where a player chooses one action regardless of the choices of any other players

▶ ▶break the game Link: https://www.youtube.com/watch?v=S0qjK3TWZE8

Sequential Games

▶ In a sequential game...
  ◇ One player takes an action (moves) and then another player takes an action (moves)
    • Once a player has taken an action, they

▶ Good for modeling
  ◇ Entry decisions for firms in an Oligopoly market
  ◇ Contract negotiations
  ◇ Tic-tac-toe

▶ We will continue to use the idea of a Nash Equilibrium

Sequential Game Setup

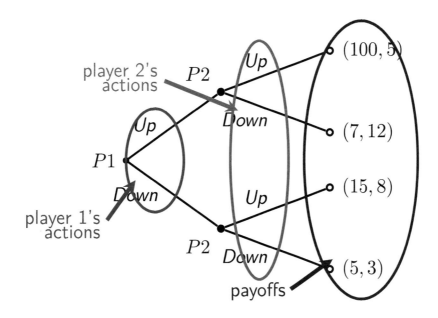

▶ Payoffs: (Player 1, Player 2)

Our First Sequential Game

Two Players: Player 1 and Player 2, with Player 1 choosing first. Both players can choose eirther to play "Up" or "Down". To find the equilibrium: **SOLVE BACKWARDS**

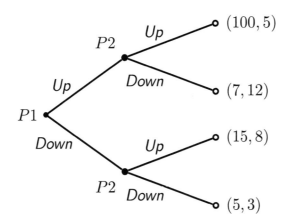

▶ Nash Equilibria?:
  ◇

An Entry Game

Two players: Firm A (price leader) and Firm B. In Stage 1, Firm A chooses a price (Low or High) and in Stage 2, Firm B chooses whether to Enter the market or Not to enter the market

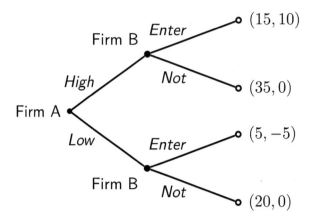

▶ Nash Equilibria?:

Entry Game Equilibrium

▶ The choice of Firm A to play the price of "Low" acts as a _____ for Firm B
  ◇ However, the lower price pushes the market closer to the competitive equilibrium than the monopoly outcome

Experiments to Test the Rationality of Economic Agents?

▶ Ultimatum Game
  ◇ Players are going to split $20
    • Player 1 chooses between an even split of $10 or $19.99 for them and $0.01 for Player 2
  ◇ If Player 2 accepts, then the players get the proposed payoffs; If player 2 rejects then both players get $0

Ultimatum Game

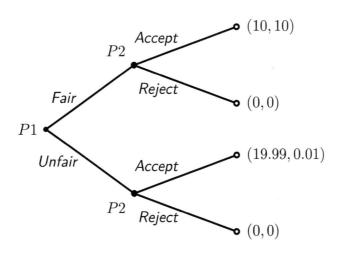

▶ Player 2 should always play:
▶ Nash Equilibria?:
   1.

Ultimatum Game Outcome

▶ Nash Equilibrium is {Unfair, Accept}
  ◇ Is this rational behavior?
  ◇ Is this realistic behavior?
    • For firms (and economists): yes
    • For non-economists: probably not
  ◇ Need to make sure that the payoffs represent the _____ – not just the monetary payoff

Dictator Game

▶ Similar to the Ultimatum Game *except* that Player 2 does not have a choice
▶ Most players that are the dictator choose a split of 60/40
  ◇ Not economists though...

Sequential Games Wrap-Up

▶ Solve sequential games backwards

▶ If the game is played repeatedly...
  ◇ The Nash Equilibrium competitive outcome can be "escaped" through bargaining or punishment just like a simultaneous game

Loyalty Plans

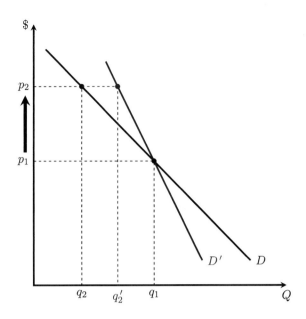

- Loyalty plans typically offer recurring customers with some additional benefit or lower prices on future purchases
  ◇ Example: frequent flyer

- Idea: make customers less sensitive to price changes
  ◇ Econ terminology: make demand less _____

Innovation

- Market power can lead to economic profits

- Firms can gain market power through product differentiation
  ◇ Reduce substitutability $\implies$ less elastic demand

- Innovation

- Trade-off for consumers
  ◇ Better products, but higher prices

Wrap-Up

▶ Oligopolies are markets where there are few firms and little, to no, product differentiation

▶ Marginal analysis is not as useful since choices are interdependent
  ◇ Trade-off between cooperation and pursuit of own interests

▶ Game theory to determine how firms maximize profits
  ◇ Look for dominant strategies and Nash equilibria

▶ Repeated games provide incentives to "escape" non-cooperative equilibria